HUMMINGBIRDS
Their Life and Behavior

HUMMINGBIRDS
Their Life and Behavior
A Photographic Study of the North American Species

Text by Esther Quesada Tyrrell

Photographs by Robert A. Tyrrell

CROWN PUBLISHERS, INC.
NEW YORK

Except where otherwise noted, drawings of birds are by D. DeGrazia and, with the exception of anatomical renderings, were made from photographs taken by Robert A. Tyrrell.

Grateful acknowledgment is hereby given to the following for permission to reprint from the following sources:

Hummingbird ranges, nesting dates, and migration patterns from *Life Histories of North American Cuckoos, Goatsuckers, Hummingbirds and Their Allies* by Arthur Cleveland Bent, copyright © 1964 by A. C. Bent. Used by permission of Dover Publications, Inc.

Hummingbird-pollinated Wildflowers listing from pp. 267–72 of *The Hummingbirds of North America* by Paul A. Johnsgard, copyright © 1983 by Smithsonian Institution, Washington, D.C. Used by permission of Smithsonian Institution Press.

Latin names for hummingbirds from *Reference List of the Birds of the World* by J. J. Morony, W. J. Bock, and J. Ferrand, Jr., copyright © 1975 by American Museum of Natural History, New York.

Published by Crown Publishers, Inc., One Park Avenue, New York, New York 10016, and simultaneously in Canada by General Publishing Company Limited

Designed by Rhea Braunstein
Manufactured in Japan

LIBRARY OF CONGRESS CATALOGING IN PUBLICATION DATA

Tyrrell, Esther Quesada
Hummingbirds: their life and behavior.

Bibliography: p.
Includes index.
1. Hummingbirds. 2. Birds—North America. I. Tyrrell, Robert A.
II. Title.
QL696.A558T87   1984   598.8'99   84-3231
ISBN 0-517-55336-8

10   9   8   7   6   5   4   3   2   1

First Edition

This book is lovingly dedicated to our parents:

Graciela Tapia de Quesada　　*Stella E. Tyrrell*
Francisco G. Quesada　　　　*Ronald A. Tyrrell*
(1918–1971)

Contents

Preface   ix

1 An Introduction to Hummingbirds   1

2 A Portfolio of North American Hummingbirds   5

3 Anatomy   39

   Bill   39

   Circulatory and Lymphatic System   40

   Digestive System   41

   Eyes   43

   Glandular System   45

   Muscular System   46

   Nervous System   47

   Reproductive System   48

   Respiratory System   49

   Skeletal System   52

   Smell   53

   Taste   53

   Tongue   54

Touch   56

Urological System   56

Voice   57

4   Feathers   59

5   Flight   85

6   Courtship and Nesting   101

Display   102

Nests   105

The Clutch   111

Nestlings   113

7   Food and Metabolism   133

8   Behavior   151

9   Wildflower Pollination   173

Hummingbird Flower Mites   182

Hummingbird-pollinated Wildflowers   184

Hummingbirds of the World   200

Bibliography   205

Index   210

Preface

Our interest in hummingbirds began in 1975 when Robert tried his hand at photographing a female Anna's Hummingbird in his mother's backyard. It was then that he discovered just how difficult photographing these tiny birds could be. Not only was the female hummingbird elusive, but her wings beat at an incredible rate and seemed to make "stopping" them on film next to impossible. The photographs in this book represent several years of enormous difficulty and expense and over 30,000 miles of travel—an endeavor that also required tremendous quantities of patience and perseverance that were ultimately necessary to surmount the photographic challenges only hinted at by that little female years ago.

As friends became aware of our interest in hummingbirds, they would, from time to time, mention sites where the birds could be found in abundance. In 1978 at one such location, Modjeska Canyon, California, we had the good fortune to meet Paul Ewald, an ornithologist, who in the months and years to follow willingly shared with us his vast store of knowledge, particularly with respect to the hummingbird's role in wildflower pollination.

As we grew more acquainted with the little birds, however, we discovered that many questions we had regarding their anatomy and behavior were not being answered satisfactorily by members of the scientific community. Sometimes there were two or more different explanations to our queries, and at other times, incredibly, nobody seemed to know what the answer was!

Attempts to track down literature on hummingbirds also proved unsuccessful, since of the smattering of volumes that had been printed, all except two were out of print. In addition, we were disappointed by the lack of complete and accurate scientific information found in any of these books. At around this time we began to think seriously of writing our own book, one which would make the most factual and up-to-date information on hummingbirds readily available to everyone.

We had also discovered that we were not alone in finding descriptions of hummingbirds in bird identification books difficult to decipher. "Birders" and others interested in observing the tiny birds in the field were perplexed by vague descriptions and drawings. To clear up the confusion, therefore, we felt that a chapter should be devoted to photographs of each species, for, we concluded, there could be no argument with a photograph.

The pictures in this book could not have been created without the assistance of Harold Edgerton, professor emeritus of the Massachusetts Institute of Technology. After many futile attempts to freeze hummingbird wings photographically, we one day received from Dr. Edgerton an unexpected but very welcome parcel containing the equipment necessary for success. Soon after receiving it, we were able to create our own equipment and were on our way.

Research for the text involved hundreds of hours of digging out obscure information from books that librarians told us hadn't even been looked at, much less checked out, for years. We discovered that there were many conflicting theories pertaining to hummingbird anatomy and behavior and concluded that the only way to resolve the differences accurately would be to send each chapter to the authority on each subject. Therefore, for their gracious assistance in reviewing the chapters, we would like to express special thanks to F. Lynn Carpenter, University of California at Irvine (behavior); Robert K. Colwell, University of California at Berkeley (hummingbird flower mites); Timothy H. Goldsmith, Yale University (eye); F. Reed Hainsworth, Syracuse University (anatomy, flight, food and metabolism); Peter Raven, Missouri Botanical Garden (wildflower pollination); and F. Gary Stiles, University of Costa Rica (courtship and nesting).

Grateful acknowledgment is also given to Kimball Garrett of the Los Angeles County Museum of Natural History for reading preliminary drafts, providing specimens of hummingbirds for dissection and cheerfully giving expert assistance and information whenever necessary.

We are indebted to Bill Miller of Bill Miller Photography, who, in addition to generously providing photographic equipment and unlimited use of his lab for film processing, also graciously granted Robert time off from work whenever necessary to take sudden trips to sites where elusive species had been sighted. Special thanks also to Walt Harvey for providing us with the very important schematic for the high-speed strobe unit, to Dick Watson for kindly giving us many rare electronic parts that enabled us to build not only the first strobe unit but also an essential spare one and to Brent Hollister of Holly Enterprises not only for taking the schematic and parts and creating two superb high-speed strobe units but also for making himself available on countless evenings after work to specialize them further and repair them.

Very special thanks go to the following "birders" who extended their gracious hospitality to us during many trips taken throughout the United States in search of particularly hard-to-find species: Neva Benn and Beth Terrazas (Buff-bellied Hummingbird), Bill and Margaret Davis (Broad-tailed Hummingbird), Bonnie McKinney (Lucifer Hummingbird), T. Spencer and Mabel Knight (Ruby-throated Hummingbird), Robert and Kate Scholes (Lucifer Hummingbird), Granville and Ethel Smith (Blue-throated and Magnificent hummingbirds), Ruth Newcomer (Broad-billed Hummingbird) and Anna Wainger (Broad-tailed Hummingbird).

In addition, we would like to say thank you to Stuart Pimm, University of Tennessee, for giving us advice and moral support which were sorely needed during the past year; to Roland Wauer, Great Smokey Mountain National Park, for valuable information on the Lucifer Hummingbird and for helping us cut through bureaucratic red tape; to Eric Brooks, South Coast Botanic Gardens, for assistance in seeking an Allen's Hummingbird and nest; to Herbert Kirby for furnishing us with excellent translations of German scientific journals; to Charles Walcott, Cornell University Laboratory of Ornithology, for advice on migration; and to Isabelle J. Paulsen for expert secretarial assistance.

We would like especially to acknowledge our editor, Brandt Aymar, for his expertise and patience in guiding us through the often-confusing world of book publishing, and Carl Apollonio of Crown Publishers, who had great enthusiasm for our project when it was no more than an idea and who was responsible more than anyone else for getting us started on it.

ESTHER AND ROBERT TYRRELL

Male Costa's with Ocotillo
(FOUQUIERIA SPLENDENS)

An Introduction to Hummingbirds | 1

He is called the Hum-Bird or Humming-Bird, because some say he makes a noise like a Spinning Wheel when he flies. . . .

Nehemiah Grew, M.D.
Philosophical Transactions
1693

Nature has favored the Americas with a sparkling bird whose jewellike colors and fascinating aerial acrobatics make it unique.

This colorful creature is the hummingbird, and the one you see drinking thirstily from an artificial feeder or darting from blossom to blossom is but one of approximately 338 species and 116 genera of the family Trochilidae, the smallest birds in the world. This lovely group of birds, many of which weigh less than a penny, is found only in the Western Hemisphere and ranges in size from *Calypte helena,* or the Cuban "Bee" Hummingbird, which at about $2\frac{1}{4}$ inches long is the smallest bird known to man, to *Patagona gigas,* an Andean species that is the largest of the family, measuring approximately $8\frac{1}{2}$ inches long. Except for the American Flycatcher, which boasts 367 species, the Trochilidae is the largest family of birds in this hemisphere.

From what ancient strain did hummingbirds descend? No one really knows since their remains were far too delicate to become fossilized. However, the fact that there are so many diverse species scattered throughout the Americas has led ornithologists to conclude that their mysterious beginnings were surely based in antiquity.

Hummingbirds are fascinating not only because of their brilliant metallic plumage but also because of their amazing powers of flight. They are perhaps best known for their ability to hover motionless in the air while delicately feeding, their wings beating at times at an unbelievable 78 beats per second. And while other birds can certainly fly forward, only hummingbirds can fly backward, a feat so incredible that upon hearing reports of their doing so the

Duke of Argyle, in his *Reign of Law,* proclaimed decidedly that "no bird can ever fly backwards" and went on to explain that while to the casual observer the hummingbird appeared to be doing just that, it was, in fact, *falling* backward. No doubt the duke would have been even more alarmed to discover that these delightful creatures can also fly upside down!

Since hummingbirds are found only in the New World, written accounts of them were not recorded until after Columbus discovered America. They were first cited in 1558 in the annals of early French explorers, but, unfortunately, since the main concern of these gentlemen was the discovery of gold, they are mentioned only in passing.

Although scientists of the seventeenth century produced detailed reports of hummingbirds, the eighteenth century is looked upon as the time when the first significant natural history studies were made. Many reports, including sightings by the legendary Captain Cook, aided these early naturalists in their observations of this unusual bird.

Long before the discovery of the New World, however, the hummingbird's beauty and swift flight had already made it a favorite among the Indians that inhabited the new territory. Frequent mention of the little bird in legends, songs and rituals attests to its prominent role in their lives.

The Aztecs, for example, adorned the ceremonial cloaks of Montezuma with the brilliant plumage of hummingbirds. Statues of deities, such as that of their god of war, Huitzilopochtli (whose awesome name, some say, is composed of two words meaning "a hummingbird" and "sorcerer that spits fire"), were fashioned so as to display the stunning metallic hues in the bird's feathers. Pictures depicting Aztec life, later praised by Hernando Cortez, were embroidered with the glittering skins of these birds, and Indian custom called for the embellishment of young brides with a profusion of dazzling hummingbird-feathered ornaments.

In addition, legend has it that the spirits of ancient Mexican warriors who died in battle were accompanied by the wife of the war god to the "mansion of the sun," where they were miraculously transformed into glittering hummingbirds.

Today, belief in the mythical powers of the hummingbird is still evident in some parts of Mexico. For example, the body of this little bird is considered to be a very potent love amulet, and it is believed that just holding it in one's hand or pocket will irresistibly draw the object of one's desire. In open-air markets specializing in the sale of magical herbs and potions, the lovelorn may often be seen gingerly selecting one or two battered hummingbird corpses from a canful or purchasing prepackaged birds, complete with printed prayers, encased in red silk bags. There are even cakes of "miraculous hummingbird soap" that, if used in the bath, promise to "dominate, conquer and attract" a loved one.

In addition, peddlers sometimes sell bags of powdered hummingbirds door to door in rural areas. Such an unusual item is not inexpensive, either, for the cost is 10,000 pesos (or roughly $80). Hummingbirds may also be purchased already stuffed and mounted.

The hummingbird also figured prominently in many Native American Indian accounts of Creation, particularly in stories of the Great Flood, in which it is often depicted as the bird sent out to see if the waters had subsided. The Arawaks and Warraus often referred to the hummingbird as the "doctor's bird" because of its close association with rituals of medicine men, and one of the more notable kachina spirits among the Hopi was that of Tocha, the Humming Bird. It was also known as Dátílyé by the Apache, Houpu-chee-naish-wen by the Karok, Na·na·tska by the Pima and Lutchi Herit by the Wintu.

In general, though, it appears that whenever an important task was at hand that required the utmost speed, the unassuming little hummingbird was dispatched to perform it quickly and efficiently. In some animal legends, too, the tiny bird is often depicted as a most handsome and desirable suitor, no doubt because of his exquisite plumage.

The hummingbird, with its glittering plumage, quick movements and diminutive size, fascinated those who first observed it. These distinctive qualities account for some of the imaginative names that hummingbirds have been given. Some of these, such as Glittering-throated Emerald, Golden-tailed Sapphire and Sapphire-spangled Emerald, clearly allude to their jewel-like colors. In fact, hummingbirds are so often described in terms of polished gems that in zoos throughout the world, aviaries housing them are always known as "jewel rooms."

Other names, such as our own "hummingbirds" and the Creole *murmures,* attempted to duplicate the distinctive whirring of their wings. And the Spanish may have sought to describe their slight dimensions by calling them *tominos,* a name that probably referred to a minute unit of measure in use at that time.

The Portuguese *beija flor* ("flower kisser") and the Mexican *chuparosa* ("rose sucker") no doubt referred to their curious way of feeding, while ancient Mexicans dramatically knew them as *huitzitzil, pigada* and *ourbiri*—names that denoted "rays of the sun" and "tresses of the day star."

Hummingbirds are extremely adaptable and can successfully survive all the elements, including cold, heat, aridity and humidity. For this reason, they are found as far north as Alaska and as far south as Tierra del Fuego. However, they are basically tropical and subtropical, and over half of the species are found in Ecuador and Brazil.

Curiously, they inhabit not only the vast mainlands of North and South America but also groups of islands, farther away. For example, 19 species are found in the West Indies and the Bahamas and 2 reside in the Juan Fernández group, about 400 miles off the coast of Chile in the Pacific Ocean.

They are most profuse in a 10-degree-wide region on the equator. Incredibly, they can be found thriving near the frozen Andean peaks of Chimborazo, Sangay and Cotopaxi, all well above 15,000 feet, as well as in the most humid tropical rain forest.

From the equatorial belt, we find that the number of species decreases as we move into areas of increased latitude. For example, 163 species are found near the equator, 54 in Costa Rica, 51 in Mexico and only 4 in Canada.

Whether encountered in natural surroundings, in gardens or in an aviary, the distinctive hummingbird is a decided favorite of many people because of its colorful sparkling plumage and original aerial abilities.

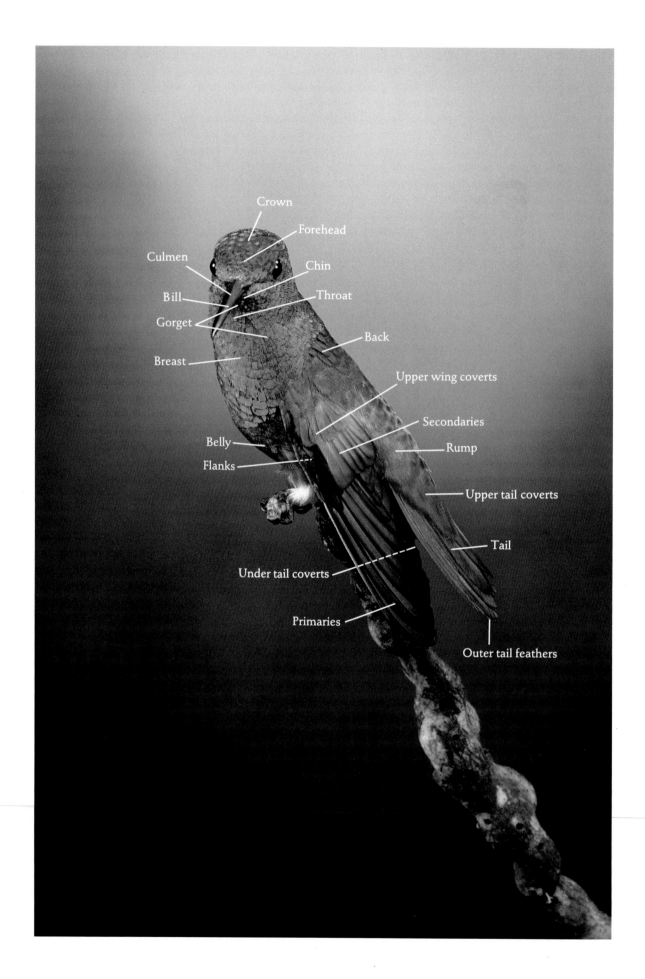

A Portfolio of North American Hummingbirds

| 2

I send you withal a little Box, with A Curiosity in it, which perhaps will be counted a trifle, yet 'tis rarely to be met with even here. It is the curiously contrived Nest of a Humming Bird, so called from the humming noise it maketh whilst it flies. 'Tis an exceeding litle Bird, and only seen in Summer, and mostly in Gardens, flying from flower to flower, sucking Honey out of the flowers as a Bee doth; as it flieth not lighting on the flower, but hovering over it, sucking with its long Bill a sweet substance. There are in the same Nest two of that Birds Eggs. Whether they use to have more at once, I know not. I never saw but one of these Nests before; and that was sent over formerly, with some other Rarities, but the Vessel miscarrying you received them not.

The Honorable John Winthrop,
Governor of Connecticut
1670

Thus went the first-known written account of a hummingbird (in this case a Ruby-throated) in the United States.

Of the 338 species of hummingbirds, only 16 breed within the boundaries of the United States. (For purposes of clarity, the definition of "United States" will be that used by the American Ornithologists Union, namely, the land bordered by Canada in the north and Mexico in the south.)

Our American species belong to 10 out of a total of 116 genera in the family Trochilidae.

Ornithologists contend that the North American species are fairly recent residents and believe this may account for their exceedingly small number.

In addition, there are 7 other species which have also been sighted north of Mexico. These additional hummers are the Antillean Crested, Bahama Woodstar, Bumblebee, Cuban Emerald, Green Violet-ear, Plain-capped Starthroat and Rufous-tailed.

Following is a dazzling portfolio of our own North American hummingbirds in all their glorious array.

Allen's Hummingbird
(SELASPHORUS SASIN). *San Pedro,
California.*

Allen's Hummingbird

GENUS *Selasphorus*

SPECIES *Selasphorus sasin*

FIELD MARKINGS Average size: 3.3–3.4 inches

The male has rufous sides, rump and tail and a glittering orange-red throat. It can be distinguished from the male Rufous, which it very closely resembles, by its green back.

It is very difficult to identify the female because of its close resemblance to the female Rufous. A comparison of the tails, however, reveals that the two outer feathers are very narrow and linear with the outer one almost bristlelike in appearance, whereas in the Rufous the four lateral tail feathers are all of normal hummingbird width and graduated in size with the outer being the smallest.

RANGE Along the coasts of California and northwestern Mexico with casual appearances in Arizona, Oregon and Washington.

BREEDING RANGE The coastal region that extends nearly the full length of California from San Clemente and the Santa Catalina Islands northward to San Francisco, Berkeley and Eureka.

WINTER RANGE North to southern California, south to central Baja California and extending into Chihuahua.

NESTING Early February to late June with the period from mid-March to late May being the height of the season.

MIGRATION Appears to start southward in August and September.

HABITAT Canyon woodlands and brush; highland meadows.

Female Allen's Hummingbird

R.D. DeGrazia

Anna's Hummingbird (CALYPTE ANNA). *El Monte, California.* NOTE: *Back view shows bird feeding from Columbine* (AQUILEGIA FORMOSA).

Anna's Hummingbird

GENUS   *Calypte*

SPECIES   *Calypte anna*

FIELD MARKINGS   Average size: 3½–4 inches

The largest California hummingbird, the adult male has a brilliant crimson helmet, gray underparts and a green back. Both sexes can be distinguished from the Rufous, Allen's and Broad-tailed by the entire absence of rufous coloring in the plumage. In size and general appearance it is most like the Broad-tailed, but their ranges are separate.

The upper parts of the adult female are darker green above than those of the male, and its underparts are grayer. There is usually a central patch of scattered red feathers on the throat. Otherwise, it is generally distinguished from the Costa's, which it closely resembles, by its larger size and darker underparts and from the Black-chinned by its stouter form.

RANGE   California and Baja California. East casually in winter to Arizona and the mainland of Mexico.

BREEDING RANGE   North to northern California. East to Mount Shasta, Pyramid Peak, Big Creek, the San Bernardino Mountains and Baja California. South to northern Baja California. West to the coastal regions of Baja California and California.

WINTER RANGE   May leave the northernmost portion of its summer range. Sometimes seen in southern Arizona.

NESTING   Mid-December to mid-August with the period from late February to mid-May being the height of the season.

MIGRATION   Performs no true migration.

HABITAT   Gardens, chaparral.

Female Anna's Hummingbird

Berylline Hummingbird (AMAZILIA BERYLLINA). *La Petaca, Sinaloa, Mexico.*

Berylline Hummingbird

GENUS	*Amazilia*
SPECIES	*Amazilia beryllina*
FIELD MARKINGS	Average size: 3½ inches
	The male is a very brilliant green above with a gray or brown abdomen. Back is green above and chestnut below. Rump is purple chestnut, tail coverts are purple. The center tail feathers are purple, and the lateral tail feathers are rufous-colored with purple tips. Wings are chestnut with some rufous. Top half of the bill is black, and the lower part is reddish.
	The female is similar, although the iridescent green on the upper portion of her body does not extend as far down into the abdomen.
RANGE	Southeast Arizona, Sonora and Chihuahua southward to Chiapas and east to Veracruz. Guatemala, El Salvador and western Honduras.
BREEDING RANGE	Not available.
WINTER RANGE	Not available.
NESTING	Not available.
MIGRATION	May be migratory only in the northernmost portion of its range.
HABITAT	Highland forests and forest edges.

Female Berylline Hummingbird

Black-chinned Hummingbird
(ARCHILOCHUS ALEXANDRI). *El Monte, California.*
NOTE: *Back view shows bird feeding from Scarlet Bugler* (PENSTEMON CENTRANTHIFOLIUS).

Black-chinned Hummingbird

GENUS   *Archilochus*

SPECIES   *Archilochus alexandri*

FIELD MARKINGS   Average size: $3\frac{1}{3}$–$3\frac{3}{4}$ inches

The sides of the male's head are black, as is its chin. An iridescent violet band separates this black chin from a white collar. There is a white spot behind the eye. Its underparts are gray. It has a green back and dusky purplish-bronze tail.

The female, which is green above and grayish white underneath, is often mistaken for the female Anna's or Costa's. It is smaller than the Anna's and differs from the Costa's in the degree of green in the tail feathers. The Black-chinned's three outermost tail feathers on each side have white tips, while the lower inside portion is quite black and the upper half is a metallic bronze-green or gray.

RANGE   Western North America.

BREEDING RANGE   North to southwest British Columbia. East to western Montana, south-central Idaho, western Colorado, New Mexico and western Texas. South to southern Texas, southern Chihuahua, southern Sonora, northeastern Baja California and southern California. West to California, Oregon, Washington and southwestern British Columbia.

WINTER RANGE   Southern California, southern Guerrero and the Federal District of Mexico.

NESTING   Early April to early September, with the period from early May to early June indicating the height of the season.

MIGRATION   Arrives in Texas in early March, New Mexico in early April, Colorado in early May, Montana in mid-May, California in late March, Oregon in early April and Washington and British Columbia in early to mid-May.

Not much data is available regarding the fall migration, but times of departure include Oregon in mid-August, California in early September, Washington in mid-September and Texas in early November.

HABITAT   Chaparral, riparian groves, dry canyons near streambeds.

Female Black-chinned Hummingbird

Blue-throated Hummingbird
(LAMPORNIS CLEMENCIAE). *Portal, Arizona.*

14

Blue-throated Hummingbird

GENUS *Lampornis*

SPECIES *Lampornis clemenciae*

FIELD MARKINGS Average size: 4½–5¼ inches

The male of this large species has an iridescent light blue throat, gray-green crown and dull gray-brown breast. There are white eye stripes on its face. Its long, broad tail has prominent white tips on the three outer feathers.

The female has gray underparts with white marks on the face and the same large blue-black tail with white corners.

RANGE Southeastern Arizona, southwestern New Mexico and Texas (Chisos Mountains). South to southern Mexico. Western Mexico north to Arizona and New Mexico.

BREEDING RANGE North to southeastern Arizona, southwestern New Mexico, southwestern Texas and Nuevo León, Mexico. East to Nuevo León and Veracruz. South to southern Veracruz, state of Mexico and Guerrero. West to central Guerrero, Durango, western Chihuahua, eastern Sonora and southeastern Arizona.

WINTER RANGE Apparently concentrated in southern Mexico, chiefly in Michoacán and Guerrero.

NESTING Mid-May to mid-July.

MIGRATION Resides in U.S. during the summer. Arrives in Texas from mid-March to late May and leaves from mid-August to late October.

HABITAT Near water in lowland canyons.

Female Blue-throated Hummingbird

Broad-billed Hummingbird
(CYNANTHUS LATIROSTRIS).
Madera Canyon, Arizona.

Broad-billed Hummingbird

GENUS   *Cynanthus*

SPECIES   *Cynanthus latirostris*

FIELD MARKINGS   Average size: 3¼–4 inches

The adult male has a glittering blue-green throat, green breast and upper parts, white underparts and a forked blue-black tail. Greenish back. Its bill is red with a dusky tip.

   The female also has a red bill with a dusky tip, grayish breast and underparts. It has a bronze-green tail.

RANGE   South from southern Arizona to central Mexico.

BREEDING RANGE   Northern to southern Arizona and probably, rarely, southwestern New Mexico and central Nuevo León. East to western Nuevo León and the state of Mexico. South to the state of Mexico, Jalisco and southern Sinaloa. West to Sinaloa, Sonora and southeastern Arizona.

WINTER RANGE   Leaves the U.S. and winters north to central Sonora. Apparently a resident in the Mexican portion of the range, it has been recorded south to Guerrero.

NESTING   Mid-April to mid-July.

MIGRATION   Arrives in Arizona in mid-March and the Santa Catalina Mountains in early April and leaves Arizona from mid-September to early October.

HABITAT   Arid canyons and slopes.

Female Broad-billed Hummingbird

Broad-tailed Hummingbird
(SELASPHORUS PLATYCERCUS).
Mount Lemmon, Arizona. NOTE:
*Back view shows bird feeding from
Beard Tongue* (PENSTEMON
BARBATUS).

Broad-tailed Hummingbird

GENUS   *Selasphorus*

SPECIES   *Selasphorus platycercus*

FIELD MARKINGS   Average size: 4–4¼ inches

The male of this Rocky Mountain species has a green crown, back and upper tail coverts and a gleaming rose-red gorget. Its middle tail feathers are greenish; the remainder are purplish-black with a bit of rufous on the outer edges. Its outer primary feathers are particularly pointed, and the wing tips are separated to produce its distinctive metallic trill, which distinguishes it from other North American hummingbirds.

The female Broad-tailed is sometimes hard to identify in the field. It is larger, though, than a Calliope and has less rufous in its tail than either it or the Rufous. In addition, its three outer tail feathers are rufous-colored at the base. There are also tinges of rufous in her flanks.

RANGE   Western U.S. and Central America.

BREEDING RANGE   North to central Nevada, northern Utah and northern Wyoming. East to eastern Wyoming, eastern Colorado, New Mexico and southwestern Texas. South to southwestern Texas, northeastern Sonora, southern Arizona, southern Nevada and east-central California. West to eastern California and western Nevada.

WINTER RANGE   Zacatecas, Jalisco, state of Mexico and Guerrero.

NESTING   Early May to late July with the period from mid-June to mid-July indicating the height of the season.

MIGRATION   Arrives in Arizona in late March, in New Mexico in early April, in Colorado during late April, Utah in early May and Wyoming in late May.

Leaves Wyoming in early September, Colorado in mid-September and New Mexico in early October.

HABITAT   Mountain meadows and glades, open vegetation, thickets.

Female Broad-tailed Hummingbird

Buff-bellied Hummingbird
(AMAZILIA YUCATANENSIS).
Brownsville, Texas.
NOTE: *Back view shows bird
feeding from Banana flower* (MUSA
X PARADISIACA L.).

Buff-bellied Hummingbird

GENUS   *Amazilia*

SPECIES   *Amazilia yucatanensis*

FIELD MARKINGS   Average size: 4–4½ inches

This hummer has a green crown and brilliant iridescent green throat. Buff-colored belly, green back and slightly forked rufous tail with chestnut tips. Reddish bill.
The female has the same markings as the male.

RANGE   Coastal regions of southern Texas and eastern Mexico.

BREEDING RANGE   North to lower Rio Grande Valley in Texas, southward through eastern Tamaulipas, eastern San Luis Potosí, Veracruz and Yucatán, Cozumel Island to Chiapas.

WINTER RANGE   Starts south from the Rio Grande Valley to southern Tamaulipas and Veracruz in October only to return in April.

NESTING   Late March to mid-July with period from early May to early June indicating the height of the season.

MIGRATION   It is possible that they migrate southward from Texas to Tamaulipas and Veracruz.

HABITAT   Forests, citrus trees, flowering bushes.

Female Buff-bellied Hummingbird

Calliope Hummingbird (STELLULA
CALLIOPE). *Mount Pinos,
California.*
NOTE: *Back view shows bird
feeding from Columbine*
(AQUILEGIA FORMOSA).

22

Calliope Hummingbird

GENUS *Stellula*

SPECIES *Stellula calliope*

FIELD MARKINGS Average size: 2.8–3.5 inches

This is the smallest bird in North America. The male has long metallic magenta feathers that extend across its white gorget. It has a gold-green back and brownish-gray tail feathers.

Aside from its minute size, the female can be distinguished from the Rufous, Black-chinned and Broad-tailed females by comparing the degree of rufous color found in its tail. The innermost pair of tail feathers are the only ones that do not have rufous at the base.

RANGE Western North America and Mexico.

BREEDING RANGE North to southern British Columbia and southwestern Alberta. East to southwestern Alberta, Montana, northwestern Wyoming, Utah and northern Baja California. South to northern Baja California and southern California. West to western California, Oregon, Washington and British Columbia.

WINTER RANGE Michoacán, Mexico, and Guerrero.

NESTING Late May to late July with the period from mid- to late June being the height of the season.

MIGRATION Starts arriving in California in early March, Oregon in early May, Washington in late April and British Columbia from late April to early May.

Leaves Washington in mid-August, Idaho in late August, Montana in early September and California from early to mid-September.

HABITAT Wooded canyons, mountains in the higher elevations, open grasslands.

Female Calliope Hummingbird

24

Costa's Hummingbird (CALYPTE COSTAE). *Palm Desert, California.* NOTE: *Front view shows bird feeding from Chuparosa* (BELOPERONE CALIFORNICA); *back view shows bird feeding from Hedgehog Cactus* (ECHINOCEREUS TRIGLOCHIDIATUS).

Costa's Hummingbird

GENUS	*Calypte*
SPECIES	*Calypte costae*
FIELD MARKINGS	Average size: 3–3½ inches

The adult male has a full helmet of glistening amethyst, and its gorget feathers extend outward to the sides. Light gray underneath, it has a green back and dusky green tail feathers.

Except for the light, purplish spots on her throat, it is almost impossible to distinguish a female Costa's from a female Black-chinned in the field. Close comparison of the tail, however, shows that the Costa's has center tail feathers that are bronze-green with the next pair similar but with black lower portions. The third pair have white tips and on the inside portion are pale brown at the base and black toward the tip with a section of iridescent green between. The fourth pair have wider white tips, more extensive gray at the base and a minimum of iridescent green separating the gray from the black.

RANGE	Southwestern U.S. and Mexico.
BREEDING RANGE	North to southern California, southern Nevada and southwestern Utah. East to southwestern Utah, east-central Arizona and (rarely) southwestern New Mexico. South to (rarely) southwestern New Mexico, southeastern Arizona and southern Baja California. West to Baja California and California.
WINTER RANGE	North to southern California and southwestern Arizona. East to southern Arizona, Sonora and southeastern Baja California. South to southern Baja. West to Baja California and southwestern California.
NESTING	Early March to late June with the period from mid-May to early June indicating the height of the season.
MIGRATION	Migrates only short distances. Arrives in Arizona in late January and leaves by late May for California and Baja California. Returns to Arizona to spend the winter.
HABITAT	Arid washes and deserts.

Female Costa's Hummingbird

R. D. DeGrazia

Lucifer Hummingbird
(CALOTHORAX LUCIFER). *Peloncillo Mountains, New Mexico.*

Lucifer Hummingbird

GENUS *Calothorax*

SPECIES *Calothorax lucifer*

FIELD MARKINGS   Average size: 3¾ inches

The male is very similar to a Costa's Hummingbird except that its crown is grayish-green. Its brilliant amethyst gorget is elongated laterally. It has a green back and greenish-brown forked tail and is also the only North American hummingbird to have a decurved bill.

The female, which has the same distinctively curved bill, also has a rounded tail and buffy underparts.

RANGE   Southern Mexico from Jalisco south to Guerrero and east to Puebla. Accidental in southwestern Arizona, New Mexico and Texas.

BREEDING RANGE   New Mexico and Texas to Mexico.

WINTER RANGE   Not available.

NESTING   Mid-June to early July.

MIGRATION   Arrives in Texas in early March and moves to lower elevations in late August. In mid-September, leaves for Mexico.

HABITAT   Deserts, arid slopes.

Female Lucifer Hummingbird

Magnificent Hummingbird
(EUGENES FULGENS). *Portal,*
Arizona.

Magnificent (Rivoli) Hummingbird

GENUS *Eugenes*

SPECIES *Eugenes fulgens*

FIELD MARKINGS Average size: 4½–5 inches

The male of this large North American species is easily distinguished by its iridescent purple crown, brilliant green throat and green-black breast. It has a green back, and its tail is composed of dark, greenish-bronze feathers that have touches of gray at the tips.

The female is green above and duskier green below. Its underparts are speckled, and it has a dark green tail. Its three outer tail feathers also have gray tips.

RANGE Southern New Mexico and Arizona. South to Nicaragua.

BREEDING RANGE North to southeastern Arizona, southwestern New Mexico and Nuevo León, Mexico. East to Nuevo León, western Tamaulipas and Guatemala. South to Guatemala and Guerrero. West to Guerrero, state of Mexico, Durango, western Chihuahua, eastern Sonora and southeastern Arizona.

WINTER RANGE Not precisely known. Doubtful that it is found north of Guerrero. From there it is found southward casually to Nicaragua.

NESTING Early May to late July with the period from mid-June to mid-July indicating the height of the season.

MIGRATION Arrives in Arizona in early April and Texas in early April. Leaves Arizona in early November and Texas in late September.

HABITAT Canyons, forests and the highland grass fields.

Female Magnificent Hummingbird

Ruby-throated Hummingbird
(ARCHILOCHUS COLUBRIS). *Sodus Bay, New York.*

Ruby-throated Hummingbird

GENUS *Archilochus*

SPECIES *Archilochus colubris*

FIELD MARKINGS Average size: 3–3¾ inches

This is the only hummingbird found east of the Mississippi. The male has a sparkling scarlet gorget, a green back, gray-white underparts and a plainly forked brownish-black tail.

The female is similar except that it does not possess the distinctive glittering scarlet throat. Also, its unique rounded tail is clearly marked with white spots.

RANGE Eastern North America and Central America.

BREEDING RANGE North to southern Alberta (rare), southern Saskatchewan, southern Manitoba, northeastern Minnesota, southern Ontario, southern Quebec, New Brunswick, Prince Edward Island and Nova Scotia. Southward along the Atlantic Coast to Florida. South to Florida, southern Louisiana and southern Texas. West to eastern Texas, Oklahoma, Kansas, South Dakota, eastern North Dakota and Alberta (rarely).

WINTER RANGE North to southern Sinaloa, probably rarely southeastern Texas, probably rarely southern Alabama and Florida. East to Florida, Cozumel Island, Honduras, Nicaragua, Costa Rica and Panama. South to Panama, El Salvador and Guatemala. West to Guatemala, Chiapas, Oaxaca, Guerrero, western Jalisco and southern Sinaloa.

NESTING Late March to mid-June, with the period from early to mid-May indicating the height of the season.

MIGRATION Arrives in Alabama in late March, Long Island in mid-April, Washington, D.C., in mid-April, New York in late April, Connecticut and Massachusetts in early May, New Hampshire and Maine in early May, Quebec and Montreal in late April to early May and Manitoba and Saskatchewan in mid-May.

Leaves Manitoba in mid-September, Iowa in early October, Illinois in mid-October, Tennessee in late October, Louisiana in early November.

HABITAT Gardens and forests.

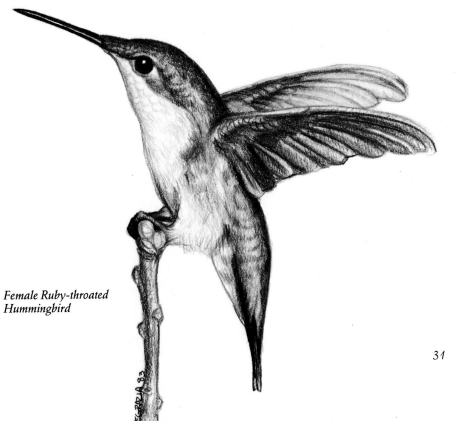

Female Ruby-throated Hummingbird

Rufous Hummingbird
(SELASPHORUS RUFUS). *Mount
Pinos, California.*
NOTE: *Both front and back views
show bird feeding from Scarlet
Penstemon* (PENSTEMON BRIDGESII).

Rufous Hummingbird

GENUS *Selasphorus*

SPECIES *Selasphorus rufus*

FIELD MARKINGS Average size: 3.3–3.9 inches

The male has extensive rufous coloring on its back (which distinguishes it from the Allen's) and an iridescent metallic copper gorget. It has a white breast and bronze-green crown and buff-colored underparts. Its rufous tail has dark tips.

The female has a green back and pale rufous sides and a lot of rufous near the base of its tail. It is extremely difficult to distinguish from a female Allen's. However, close inspection of the tails will show that the green center feathers have a lot (sometimes more than half their length) of rufous color at the base. The next two feathers have black along the lower edge and rufous at the top with green separating the two. The outer tail feathers of the Rufous are also slightly broader.

RANGE Western North America.

BREEDING RANGE North to southeastern Alaska. East to eastern Alaska, southwestern Alberta and western Montana. South to southern Montana, southern Idaho and east-central California. West to California, Oregon, Washington, western British Columbia and southeastern Alaska.

WINTER RANGE Zacatecas, Jalisco, the state of Mexico and Michoacán.

NESTING Early May to early June with the period from early May to late May indicating the height of the season.

MIGRATION Arrives in California from early to mid-February, Washington by late February, Oregon by early March, British Columbia by early April and Alaska by mid-April.

HABITAT High mountains, stream banks, forests and forest edges, chaparral, forest glades.

Female Rufous Hummingbird

Violet-crowned Hummingbird
(AMAZILIA VIOLICEPS). *La Capilla
del Taxte, Sinaloa, Mexico.* NOTE:
*Back view shows bird feeding from
Lion's ears* (LEONOTIS
NEPETIFOLIA).

Violet-crowned Hummingbird

GENUS   *Amazilia*

SPECIES   *Amazilia violiceps*

FIELD MARKINGS   Average size: $3\frac{3}{4}$–$4\frac{1}{4}$ inches

Another large North American hummer, the male of this species has an iridescent violet-blue crown and snowy white throat and underparts. Its back is gray-brown, and the tail is also gray-brown with portions dusky-colored. It has a red bill with a dusky black tip.

The female is similar but its crown is duller.

RANGE   Southeastern Arizona and southwestern New Mexico, Sonora to Chiapas.

BREEDING RANGE   Southeastern Arizona and southwestern New Mexico.

WINTER RANGE   Sonora to Chiapas.

NESTING   Not available.

MIGRATION   It is believed that the Violet-crowned Hummingbirds residing in Arizona and New Mexico during July and August migrate. Arrive in Sonora from early March.

HABITAT   Along stream banks in deep canyons, forests and forest edges and deserts.

Female Violet-crowned Hummingbird

White-eared Hummingbird
(HYLOCHARIS LEUCOTIS). *La Petaca, Sinaloa, Mexico.*

White-eared Hummingbird

GENUS *Hylocharis*

SPECIES *Hylocharis leucotis*

FIELD MARKINGS Average size: 3½ inches

The male has a red bill with a black tip and a broad white stripe behind the eye. It has a violet crown, glittering violet and emerald-green gorget, white abdomen and dark green underparts. It also has a greenish-gold back and square-tipped tail of the same color.

The female also has a red bill and a broad white stripe behind the eye. There are small spots on the throat, and it has green flanks.

RANGE Southeastern Arizona to Central America.

BREEDING RANGE Southeastern Arizona, north to central Sonora, northern Chihuahua and northern Tamaulipas. East to Tamaulipas, Veracruz, Honduras and Nicaragua. South to Nicaragua, Oaxaca and Guerrero. West to Guerrero, state of Mexico, Durango, western Chihuahua and Sonora.

WINTER RANGE Not available.

NESTING Late March through December.

MIGRATION Arrives in Texas in late April and leaves in mid-August.

HABITAT Woodlands near streams.

Female White-eared Hummingbird

SKELETAL SYSTEM

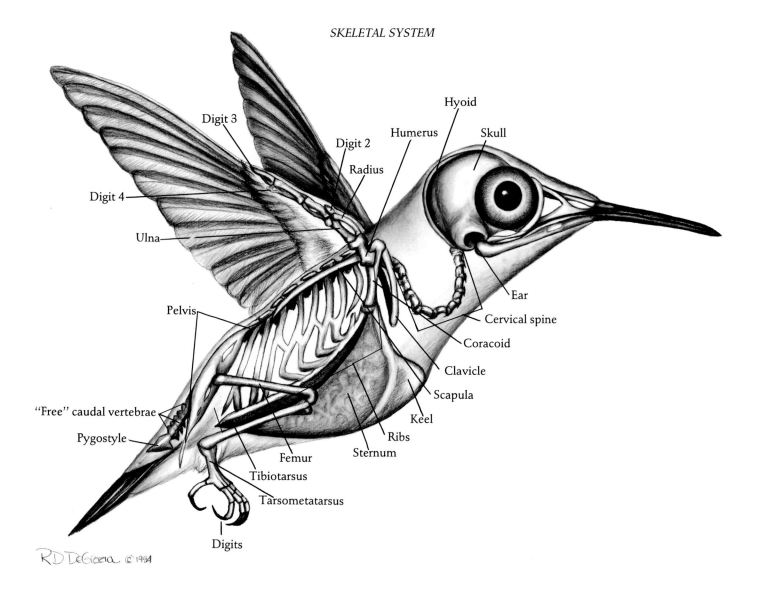

Digit 3

Digit 2

Humerus

Hyoid

Skull

Radius

Digit 4

Ulna

Ear

Cervical spine

Pelvis

Coracoid

Clavicle

Scapula

"Free" caudal vertebrae

Keel

Pygostyle

Ribs

Femur

Sternum

Tibiotarsus

Tarsometatarsus

Digits

RD DeGrazia © 1984

Anatomy

| 3

BILL

Perhaps more than any other feature, the long, slim bills of hummingbirds easily distinguish them from other birds. They are linear, taper to a fine point and are usually longer than the head. In addition, those of females are generally longer than those of males.

They are also greatly diversified, reflecting adaptation to the particular feeding habits of each species. Hummingbird bills can be straight or decurved, and some even curve upward. The longest one, that of the Sword-billed Hummingbird, is 4 inches long and almost the length of its entire body, while the shortest appears to be the $^5/_{16}$-inch bill of the Purple-backed Thornbill, whose stubby (by hummingbird standards) beak is not even as long as its head. The only hummingbird in North America with a curved bill is the Lucifer.

Bills can be red, yellow or black, but 80–90 percent are black or dusky-colored. Those of the North American species are dark, with the exception of the Berylline, Broad-billed, Buff-bellied, Violet-crowned and White-eared hummingbirds, whose beaks are either completely or partially red.

The long, narrow shape allows the bird to probe deeper into the centers of tubular flowers to reach the nectar within, and the bird's superior aerial abilities make up for the bill's slimness and the resulting small gape, which would otherwise be a liability in capturing insects.

Besides enabling the hummingbird to tap nectar located within slim blossoms, the bill is indispensable for preening, capturing insects and attack-

The needlelike bills of hummingbirds come in a variety of shapes. In North America, the Lucifer is the only hummer with a decurved bill.

The color of bills also varies. Although those of most of the North American species are black, the bills of the Violet-crowned (pictured), Buff-bellied, Broad-billed, White-eared and Berylline are either red or partly red.

ing other hummingbirds. And females are especially adept at using their bills for transporting nesting material and constructing nests.

Bills are composed of a bony center with a covering made up of cornified epidermis. The lower portion is completely covered by the upper one, protecting the sensitive tongue.

In addition, the bill is useful in determining a hummingbird's age. For example, the culmen, or ridge that runs lengthwise along the bill's upper portion, is longer in an adult than in a young bird. And the sides of the bills of juvenile hummingbirds not yet one year old have been found to be extremely corrugated. This unusual ridged texture is not seen in the yellow bills of newly born hummingbirds but appears as they grow older and their bills darken. Later, it takes nine months for the ridged bill to become smooth again.

CIRCULATORY AND LYMPHATIC SYSTEM

The cells of a bird's body require a constant supply of oxygen and nutrients. In addition, it is vital that the waste products they have produced be carried away efficiently. These important functions are carried out by the circulatory system, which is also responsible for passing waste elements to the kidneys, distributing hormones secreted by the endocrine glands, helping the bird heal itself and maintaining its temperature.

The circulatory system consists of a powerful heart and a network of tubes through which blood travels to the tissues of the body.

The weight of a hummingbird's heart ranges from approximately 1.75 to 2.5 percent of its total body weight and is, relatively speaking, the largest among all animals. The more diminutive species of hummingbirds have proportionately larger hearts than the bigger ones. Relatively large hearts among hummingbirds are necessary because of the combination of an extremely rapid metabolism and a method of feeding that requires them to fly a great deal.

The body of a hummingbird does not contain much blood. What little it has is, as in other birds, distributed throughout the body in two ways. The first, venous blood, carries carbon dioxide that is transported from the capillaries to the heart, while arterial blood comes from the heart and lungs.

Venous blood is handled only by the right side of the heart, and arterial blood, which is bright red, is handled only by the left side. The blood of birds contains corpuscles, also known as erythrocytes, plasma and other materials such as salts and other chemicals. Their blood also contains the greatest concentration of erythrocytes per unit of volume. The blood of the Ruby-topaz Hummingbird, for example, was found to contain 6,590,000 per cubic millimeter. These cells are smaller but have been found to contain more hemoglobin.

The heart has four chambers: two auricles and two ventricles. It is a muscular organ that pumps blood to the body through arteries and back to it through veins.

Venous blood enters the right auricle through three major veins: the postcaval and two precaval. From there it passes into the right ventricle and on to the pulmonary artery, which bifurcates, with each section going to one lung.

In the lungs, blood that is rich in carbon dioxide undergoes an exchange process and leaves the lungs filled with oxygen. Blood then passes to the left auricle by means of the pulmonary veins and is pumped to the left ventricle and out of the heart through the right aortic arch. In a study involving over 30 hummingbirds, it was found that not only the left but also the right systemic (or fourth aortic arch) was absent. In its place, the right ductus caroticus transported blood to the abdominal aorta. This is another anatomical peculiarity of hummingbirds. Blood then travels to the body tissues through the arteries.

The innominates, specialized arterial vessels that take blood to the pectorals and brachials, are larger and have thicker walls than the other blood vessels. The smallest vessels are the capillaries, which transport nutrients and oxygen to the body's cells and take away waste materials.

The lymphatic system, similar to the circulatory system, moves waste and fats through the body and aids the bird in combating disease. These substances are transported through tubes in the form of a plasmalike liquid called lymph, which is ultimately emptied into the bloodstream.

When resting, a hummingbird's heart beats approximately 500 times per minute. However, this rate can go up to over 1,200 times per minute when the bird is excited. Compare this to a low of 38 and a high of 176 times per minute for an ostrich!

A hummingbird's temperature ranges from 104° to 110° F, with the norm being approximately 105° F. Its body temperature at night is approximately 70° F, although when the temperature outside is extremely low, it has the ability to enter torpor by lowering its breathing and heart rate and total metabolism.

DIGESTIVE SYSTEM

The purpose of digestion is to separate nutrients from ingested food in order to nourish the body's tissues. Elements that are not immediately utilized are either stored by the body for future use or excreted.

Hummingbirds, which have the most rapid metabolism of all birds, consume the greatest amount of food, relative to their body weight, of any vertebrate, and they burn up energy very quickly. Their digestive systems seem designed to break down food as quickly as possible in order to pass it into the bloodstream and on to the body tissues. This rapid cycle also allows for speedy elimination of waste products, thus freeing the bird from extra weight. The vital organs of this system are located in the center of the hummingbird, permitting balanced flight.

DIGESTIVE SYSTEM

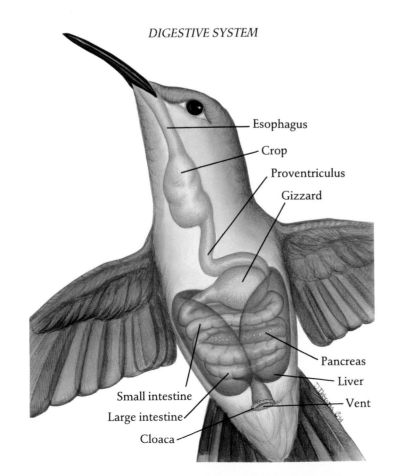

Esophagus

Crop

Proventriculus

Gizzard

Pancreas

Liver

Vent

Small intestine

Large intestine

Cloaca

The digestive system of hummingbirds, like those of other birds and mammals, is really no more than a large tube extending from mouth to cloaca. In the mouth are found few taste buds and the most rudimentary of salivary glands. Food, which is swallowed quickly, passes down the extremely thin, flexible walls of the gullet or esophagus to the crop, a saclike distension where food is both moistened and softened.

The crop is often found to contain either nectar or insects, and it has been suggested that it serves as an important alimentary cache, the contents of which enable the bird to maintain a constant temperature on cold nights. Food in the crop of a Magnificent Hummingbird takes approximately 30 to 40 minutes to pass into the stomach.

The stomach is next, and it is divided into two parts—the proventriculus and the ventriculus (or gizzard). It is in the soft proventriculus that the first major chemical breakdown of food occurs—in this instance by gastric juices.

The ventriculus, or gizzard, which in most birds is larger than the proventriculus and contains sharp particles such as gravel or sand to aid in breaking the food into small bits, is small in the hummingbird; most of a hummingbird's diet consists of either nectar or soft insects, which can be digested adequately in the proventriculus. Also, in other birds it is a ridged, heavy organ that is lined with hard tissue, while in the hummingbird its structure more closely resembles that of a stomach. Its walls secrete mucus.

From the ventriculus, food passes to the duodenum or upper end of the small intestine, where bile from the liver and enzymes from the pancreas further break down the food. Nutrients are absorbed through the walls of the small intestine into the bloodstream.

The small intestine of the Ruby-throated Hummingbird is 2 inches long (that of the ostrich is 46 feet long). Its diminutive length reflects the bird's easily digestible diet—the more complex the diet, the longer the intestine must be.

Bile from the liver enters the small intestine through ducts in its walls and works to neutralize acids and emulsify fats.

In addition to producing bile, the large, two-lobed liver also stores lipids (fats) and glycogen. While the liver is generally a dark brown color, those of high-altitude hummingbirds often appear creamy white because of the large amounts of lipids contained in them, often reaching levels of 15–30 percent of total liver weight.

The amount of liver lipid in hummingbirds has been measured at 6 percent in tropical species versus 11–15 percent in the Ruby-throated Hummingbird. The amount of lipids in the liver of a Ruby-throated Hummingbird readying itself for its marathon migratory flight across the Gulf of Mexico measured 41–46 percent compared to its normal level of 13 percent.

It has been suggested that the level of lipids in the hummingbird's liver is great because of the high metabolic rate and its sugary diet.

Enzymes such as amylase, trypsin and lipase are secreted by the pancreas into the small intestine through ducts and specifically break down carbohydrates, proteins and fats. Within the pancreas are the islets of Langerhans, which secrete insulin.

Curiously, the hummingbird does not have paired caeca, fingerlike projections that further act on food bacteriologically and that are usually located between the two intestines. Their absence has mystified ornithologists for many years. Hummingbirds also lack gall bladders.

Food continues on to the large intestine, which is relatively short, digestion being nearly completed by the time food reaches it. Ducts from the kidneys and reproductive organs empty into it and solid waste products pass through it to the cloaca, the common channel for the digestive, excretory and reproductive systems. This waste matter exits the body through the vent.

The dark, immovable eyes of the hummingbird are situated high on its head, a location which allows the bird to see an enemy striking from above.

Relatively speaking, a bird's eyes are larger than those of mammals (just consider the huge size of their orbits) and both eyes may even outweigh the brain. The fact that a hummingbird's eyes are set on the sides of its head increases the bird's total visual field, and it can consequently see both what is on the side (monocular vision) and what is in front (binocular vision).

The shape of the hummingbird's eye is globose, unlike the flat eye of the swan or the tubular one of the owl. Each is 6–8 millimeters in diameter (an ostrich's eye is 50 millimeters in diameter).

The anatomical structure of the hummingbird's eye does not differ greatly from that of other birds' eyes.

The hard outside portion of the eyeball, the sclera, is a firm membrane that protects the eyeball and maintains its form. The black vascular choroid, situated just in front of the sclera, supplies the rods and cones of the retina with nutritive elements. The next layer is the retina, the lining inside the eyeball, which is composed of an outer pigmented layer and an inner layer of nerves called the retina proper, which, in turn, is made up of nerve cells and fibers and Müller's cells (a supporting framework). Relative to the size of the whole eye, a bird's retina is almost twice the size of man's but in comparison to it does not have a very substantial supply of blood.

The cornea, the outermost front portion of the eyeball, is made up of the tissues of the sclera. The curve of the cornea is controlled by Crampton's muscle. Behind the cornea is the aqueous humor, a liquid that fills in the space

DORSAL VIEW OF THE LEFT EYE

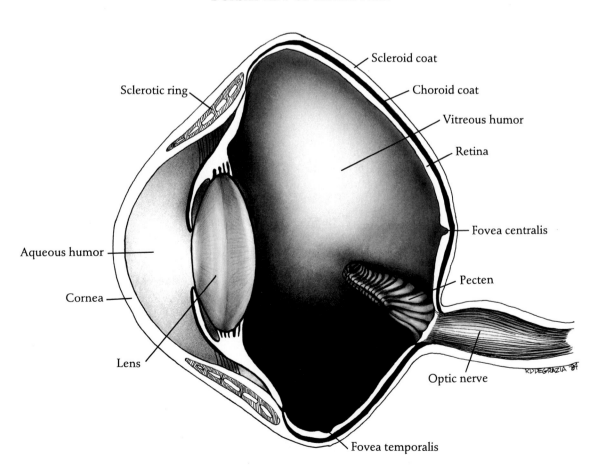

Scleroid coat

Sclerotic ring

Choroid coat

Vitreous humor

Retina

Fovea centralis

Aqueous humor

Pecten

Cornea

Lens

Optic nerve

Fovea temporalis

between it and the lens, a structure that is clear and delicately fibered. The ciliary body, made up of a combination of the layers of the choroid and retina, holds the lens in place. Between the lens and retina is the vitreous humor. In front of the lens is the iris, also composed of the layers of the choroid and retina. The iris regulates the amount of light entering the eye by enlarging or closing the pupil. It is made up of striated muscles, which are more effective than smooth ones, and for this reason the bird's pupils open and close very quickly. Behind the iris there is usually a black layer; if this layer is missing, the eye has a blue color.

Within the vitreous humor and just in front of the optic nerve is a curious-looking organ with brushlike projections called the pecten. Its blood vessels are larger than capillaries and its multipleated structure seems to indicate an attempt to pack as much blood as possible into a little space. It has been theorized that the pecten makes up for the lack of vascularity in the retina and transports blood to it through the vitreous humor. A further suggestion is that the pecten casts a shadow on the retina, alerting the bird to movement nearby.

Visual cells, or receptors, are specialized cells found in the retina. There are two kinds—rods and cones. There is a high ratio of these cells to the fibers of the optic nerve. The more closely packed the visual cells, the greater the acuity.

The rods, which contain rhodopsin, deal with colorless and dim light, providing great sensitivity to it but not much acuity. Cones, on the other hand, deal with color and bright light vision. They provide for greater acuity, or ability to see color and detail, and are less sensitive than rods. Hummingbirds, which are active by day, probably have a lot of cones and few rods.

The cones contain colored oil droplets. Except for their ability to filter out light at short wavelengths, the function of these droplets is not yet exactly known. Different species of birds have droplets ranging in color from yellow to orange, red and sometimes green. In the hummingbird, however, these oil droplets are at least two shades of yellow and red and may serve to heighten the contrast of light-colored objects in the blue sky.

The belief that hummingbirds seek out red because they can detect infrared rays is simply not true.

There are two areas in the retinas of hummingbirds (along with kingfishers, bitterns and a few other types of birds) where vision is particularly acute. Here there are very large numbers of cones but no rods. The first, the fovea centralis, is situated near the center of the eye. This round indentation or de-

A transparent nictitating membrane (or third eyelid) completely covers and protects the exposed eyeball when the bird flies into the wind.

pression creates a greater area to allow more cones. The refractive index (or power to bend light) of the fovea centralis is distinct from that of the vitreous humor, which precedes it. Hummingbirds have a greater visual acuity because the magnification at this point can be as much as 30 percent. The bird uses this particularly sharp area of vision when it looks straight out to the side. It has been suggested that when it cocks its head it is attempting to image the object it is looking at on this fovea. The fovea centralis is sometimes called the "search" fovea, since it aids the bird in distinguishing objects in green areas.

There is also a fovea temporalis that is found near the rear margin of the retina. This fovea is used by the bird when it is looking straight ahead and utilizing its binocular vision. It is not connected to the central fovea, nor is it as deep. It is called the "pursuit" fovea and is helpful when the bird is chasing insects.

All that a bird sees at one time is in focus because of the shape of its eyeball. Changing of focus is known as accommodation, and birds focus their eyes by changing the shape of the lens, an action that is accomplished by squeezing the ciliary body.

In addition to its opaque eyelids, the hummingbird, like other birds, also has a nictitating membrane, which is sometimes called the third eyelid. This transparent membrane completely covers the exposed eye and protects it when the bird is flying into the wind. The nictitating membrane also cleanses and moistens the cornea during the day.

GLANDULAR SYSTEM

The hummingbird, like other birds, has two types of glands—those with ducts and those without. The ductless glands, which are also called endocrine glands, secrete substances directly into the blood or lymph.

These secretions, or hormones, circulate through the bloodstream and affect mental, chemical and physical functions such as growth and behavior. There is a close interrelationship between them and the many other systems of the bird's body. The chief endocrine glands are the pituitary, thyroid, parathyroids, adrenals and pancreas. The thymus is no longer considered an endocrine gland.

The pituitary gland is located within the skull at the base of the brain. It is often referred to as the master gland, because its secretions regulate those of the rest of the body. One lobe of this gland secretes the thyrotropic hormone, which controls the thyroid gland; gonadotropic hormones, which regulate the activities of the sexual organs; and adrenocorticotropic hormone, which is directly concerned with the adrenals. Vasopressin, pitressin and oxytocin, secreted by the other lobe, increase blood pressure, impede the urine flow and may cause premature egg laying, respectively.

The thyroid is a paired gland situated at the base of the neck. It secretes thyroxine, which is intricately involved in both the development of feathers and the molting process. An overabundance of this hormone will cause a bird to molt faster and to develop dark feathers with an inordinate amount of barbules. It also is involved in regulating the bird's metabolic rate, sexual and growth processes and body temperature.

The levels of phosphorus and calcium in the blood are regulated by the parathyroids.

Glands in the pancreas are known as the pancreatic islets and secrete two major hormones—insulin, which influences sugar uptake from the blood, and glucagon, which influences the breakdown of fats and glycogen.

Male gonads produce androgens, while those of the female produce estrogens. Estrogen originates in the ovary and stimulates the development and regulation of the female bird's sexual organs and breeding behavior. In addition, the hummingbird's gonads also secrete such hormones as progesterone and testosterone.

The thymus gland is located underneath the neck tissues and shrinks as the bird gets older. Although in mammals it is involved in the animal's immune system, its function in birds is unknown.

Secretin, a hormone that regulates pancreatic juices, is produced by the small intestine.

In times of fight or flight, the adrenals, by their secretion of adrenaline, provide increased energy by speeding up the heart, furnishing the blood with more sugar and raising the blood pressure. These yellow-orange glands are located underneath the kidneys.

The chief skin gland is the uropygial gland, which has two lobes, is cone-shaped and is found near the base of the tail. It may be coupled with a small group of feathers whose function is to draw up the oil by capillary action like a wick. During preening, the hummingbird touches its bill to this gland, and the oil it collects may have several functions. These include keeping the bill and legs lubricated, dressing or conditioning the feathers and waterproofing the feathers. It has also been suggested that the oily secretion from this gland contains vitamin D, which the bird consumes as it preens.

MUSCULAR SYSTEM

The muscular system of a hummingbird enables it to move. The very act of flying, during which the bird's entire body is supported by its wings, is a complex process that alone requires dozens of muscles. The muscles of the wings and tail work together and make many adjustments when the bird is flying or performing its extraordinary aerial feats.

Each feather on a bird's body is connected to a muscle, and such movements as feather fluffing and ruffling during bathing and drying off, during display and for purposes of temperature regulation, are all made possible by these cutaneous muscles.

There are basically two kinds of muscles—dark and light. Dark muscle is a deep red and contains a great many capillaries. A chicken, which is incapable of flying for sustained periods of time, has lighter-colored pectoral muscles than the hummingbird, which is a powerful flier, adept at sustained flight, and has pectoral muscles of the dark and richly vascular variety. Dark muscles contain fat, which is easily stored and is used to sustain muscular movement, as well as lipase, which breaks down fat. Dark muscle tissue is also made up of red fibers that are small in diameter and have large numbers of mitochondria, myoglobin and enzymes.

Sudden bursts of energy are best handled by white-meated muscles. White tissue, which consists of broad fibers, contains glycogen, which gives the bird quick energy when needed, and small amounts of fat.

There are two chief muscles involved in flying. The first, the pectoralis major, is attached to the sternum, clavicle and humerus and is used in pulling the wing down, a movement that also propels the bird forward. In most birds this muscle is quite a bit larger (sometimes up to ten times larger) than the second muscle, the supracoracoideus, which raises the wing. However, since the raising of the wing is also an extremely strong movement in hummingbird flight, its supracoracoideus is about one-half the size of the pectoralis major.

The supracoracoideus is located directly beneath the pectoralis major. It, too, is attached to the sternum. It raises the wings by means of a rope-and-pulley-type structure that involves a tendon running from the supracoracoideus through a notch or hole between the bones of the shoulder.

There are certain peculiarities found in the muscular structure of hummingbirds that distinguish them from other birds. For example, in other strong fliers, the pectoralis major and supracoracoideus make up about 15–25 percent of their entire body weight. And in other weaker-flying birds the pectoral muscles are even smaller. In the hummingbird, however, the percentage is higher—approximately 21–35 percent. Also, the supracoracoideus is proportionately heavier than in other birds.

As mentioned before, within the pectoral muscles are mitochondria. These are organelles of the cell that are its chief energy source. White fibers have little and sometimes no mitochondria at all, while more are found in the red variety. The narrow red fibers of the hummingbird's pectoral muscles have great amounts of mitochondria that are so large they have been referred to as "giant-sized" by some scientists.

Scientists have found that the same narrow dark red fat-loaded fiber is found in both the pectoralis major and supracoracoideus of the Ruby-throated Hummingbird with no indication of white or any other type of fiber. Because the fibers take up less space, it is believed that a greater area is available for a larger amount of nutrient and gas exchange.

Some other birds also have identical fibers in both of their pectorals, but the anatomical structure of the Ruby-throated Hummingbird is unique in that all of these fibers are red. Even more astonishing, however, is the fact that the fibers of this species' supracoracoideus are smaller than those of its pectoralis major—a fiber construction that is truly unusual in the avian world.

NERVOUS SYSTEM

The nervous system is an arrangement of special cells that communicate with each other and transmit information to the body from the outside world as well as within the organism.

It is made up of two parts—the central system, which is composed of the brain and spinal cord, and the peripheral system, which is composed of afferent and efferent nerves.

The brain of a bird is larger in proportion to its body than that of any other vertebrate except mammals and is contained in a small bony case just behind the orbits. It is the center for the important nerves of the head, and it is within it that impulses from the body are deciphered. Some responses originate here, while some are stored for future use, and it controls the voluntary movements of the body. Impressions from the outside world are transmitted by afferent nerves to the brain, where they are interpreted, and corresponding orders are sent to the glands or muscles by efferent nerves.

The cerebral hemispheres make up the largest part of the brain. Those of the hummingbird are quite small and have been described as "primitive." In structure they have been found, in some species at least, to be more like those of reptiles than of birds.

The larger the portion of the brain that controls a particular organ, the more important the organ is to the creature. For example, since acute vision is vital to the hummingbird, its optical lobes are large. And the part of the brain that deals with hearing is also well developed.

It is not surprising that the cerebellum is large and well developed, with a great many folds, since it deals with the various functions of movement that are vital to an animal with the powerful flight of the hummingbird. Its size also reflects the fact that the bird is capable of intricate aerial movements. Anatomically speaking, it extends farther in front of the optic lobes than it does in other birds. Located behind the cerebral hemispheres, it also controls reflex action and equilibrium.

The cerebral cortex, which controls learned behavior, is small. Instinctive behavior is regulated by the cerebrum, which is large and quite smooth in texture. The hummingbird's corpus striatum, the portion of the brain involved in behavior that cannot be changed or modified, is proportionately smaller than those of other birds.

The spinal cord, for the most part, is similar to those of other birds. The ventral gray columns in the cervical area are exceptionally large, but this is not unexpected, considering the hummingbird's highly developed flight musculature.

The peripheral system—the system of afferent and efferent nerves—controls the vital organs of the body. The afferent portion of this system responds to sensations of the heart, lungs and other organs, and the efferent portion (also known as the autonomic nervous system) stimulates them.

The autonomic nervous system is further divided into two parts—sympathetic and parasympathetic. The sympathetic nervous system regulates the bird's reactions during stressful situations (the fight or flight reaction). It expands blood vessels in the muscles, retards digestive processes, quickens the heart rate and the release of adrenaline.

The parasympathetic nervous system, on the other hand, is utilized by the bird when it is in a calmer state and provides for the opposite reaction, such as quickening digestive action, lowering the heart rate and allowing blood to flow through blood vessels at a normal pace.

REPRODUCTIVE SYSTEM

Hummingbirds, like all other birds, are oviparous, which means that they lay eggs.

The gonads, or sexual organs, are small and lie dormant for most of the year, enlarging only during the breeding season. (The hummingbird's reproductive system is pictured in the drawing on p. 56.)

During coitus, the male hummingbird mounts the female's back and presses his cloaca against hers, expelling sperm into her oviduct.

The male has a pair of pale oval testes located near the kidneys. The left testis is sometimes larger than the right. Testes recrudesce (enlarge) to several hundred times their normal size when the birds are in their breeding cycle. Each has a very coiled sperm duct, known as the vas deferens, which leads to the cloaca. Its lower portion, the seminal vesicle, acts as a storage receptacle for sperm and sometimes bulges before the breeding season.

Paired ovaries begin to develop in a female hummingbird, but early in development the right one degenerates, leaving her with only the left one. It is believed that retaining only one ovary and oviduct saves her from carrying unnecessary weight.

There are a great many ova, or egg cells, in the ovary of a female hummingbird, as in the ovaries of other female birds, and a small number ripen during the breeding season. Those that do form a yolk and, when fully ripened, break through the follicle covering and begin to travel down the oviduct. Both ciliary and muscular action aid the ovum in its journey.

At copulation, which occurs most frequently during the early breeding cycle, thousands of mobile sperm enter the cloaca and begin their ascent into the upper portion of the oviduct. Only one, however, will penetrate each ovum. The fertilized ovum, or germ cell, is the egg's nucleus. When the ovum reaches the midpoint of the oviduct, it receives a thick coating of albumen (egg white), which is secreted by glands in this area.

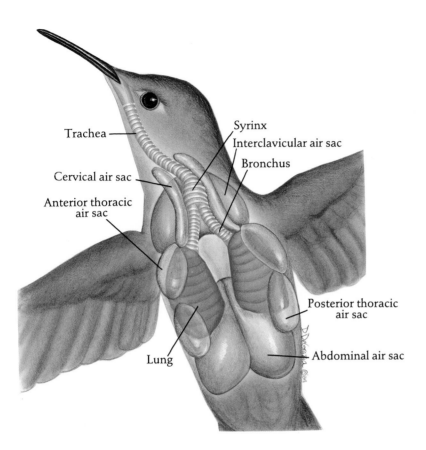

Two layers of shell membrane, which prevent evaporation, are deposited by glands in the walls of the lower portion of the oviduct, which is known as the uterus. The shell, which supports the fragile embryo, hardens as soon as it passes out of the body via the vent.

RESPIRATORY SYSTEM

The respiratory system is made up of organs that are specialized for the intake of oxygen and the elimination of carbon dioxide. Birds, which are extremely active, have the greatest oxygen requirements among vertebrates, and they may have the most highly evolved respiratory system of all animals. This system has adapted to allow great quantities of oxygen to be utilized by a relatively small body.

Some birds breathe at an incredibly fast rate. For example, a resting hummingbird breathes 250 times per minute compared to 25–30 times for a pigeon and 16 times for man. When excited, a hummingbird's respiratory rate rises to 273 times per minute.

The organs of the respiratory system consist of two compact lungs and a network of air sacs. Air enters the body of a hummingbird through its nostrils and continues on to the internal nares and the pharynx.

Situated behind the base of the tongue is the glottis, a long slit that allows air to pass into the windpipe. An epiglottis (the protective cartilage flap that prevents foreign matter from entering the windpipe in man) is absent in birds. The glottis compresses shut by a very rapid reflex action. Air passes from the glottis to the larynx, which is located at the upper end of the trachea.

Although it is the location of the vocal apparatus in mammals, the larynx is not a specialized organ for voice in birds; instead it acts as a passageway for air leading to the windpipe.

The trachea, or windpipe, is made up of bony rings in front and cartilaginous rings in back. These rings give it both support and maximum flexibility to accompany the great flexibility of the cervical spine. The bony portion strengthens and protects an area that is otherwise not well protected while the sternum and cervical spine protect the upper portion of the trachea, which is made up of more pliable cartilage. The area between the rings is composed of a very elastic membrane. The trachea travels downward just in front of the esophagus but detours at the crop and passes through the wishbone. At this point, it bifurcates into two tubes, called bronchi, each of which proceeds to a lung. At this junction is found the syrinx, which is the bird's organ of voice.

Each bronchus looks like a trachea that has been cut in half, with inner walls that are membraneous and smooth and outer walls that are made up of rings. The bronchi lead into the tiny pink lungs, which are snugly fitted on either side of the bird's backbone. This portion of the bronchus is called the mesobronchus. The mesobronchi separate further into dorsobronchi and ventrobronchi and connect, finally, with parabronchi, which are the main membranes utilized in respiration. They transport air to the anterior thoracic, interclavicular and cervical sacs.

All the parts of the respiratory system are ultimately connected by the parabronchi, which are minute capillary vessels. There are approximately 1,000 small membranes or parabronchi, and it is here that the exchange of gases takes place.

Since the lungs are not very elastic, they cannot expand a great deal; they can also only hold so much air. Nature, however, provided the bird with air sacs that enable it to inhale even more air. All space within the bird's body that is not utilized by organs or other tissues is filled by the nine air sacs, which hold air and are used in conjunction with lungs to help maintain the lightness of the body. The air sacs may also serve to cool the body.

These sacs are bladders of a delicate filmy texture, not particularly vascular, and originate at the lungs. They are found throughout the body, fitting snugly into the spaces between and surrounding the organs. It has been sug-

A hummingbird cools off by an internal evaporative cooling system that takes in fresh air by panting. These hot Blue-throated, (OPPOSITE), Anna's (ABOVE) and Magnificent (BELOW), hummers were photographed when outside temperatures were over 105° F.

gested that air sacs momentarily hold air while the bird is in flight and singing.

There are two pairs of air sacs in the thoracic cavity, one pair in front of the other. Two subscapular air sacs are found under each scapular, and two axillary air sacs are located underneath each wing at the point where it joins the pectoral girdle. This last pair is connected to the interclavicular air sac, which is located along the neck. The overall function of the air sacs, which are connected to the lungs by tubes, is to increase the efficiency of respiration and to help control the temperature of the bird's body.

The process of inhalation passes a small portion of air to the air tubules in the lungs, where carbon dioxide in the blood is exchanged for oxygen. The majority of the inhaled air, however, is transported to air sacs through the lungs for temporary storage. Upon exhalation, air is passed back to the cells of the lungs, where the exchange of gases takes place and where blood is oxygenated. Water and carbon dioxide are the waste products that are eventually exhaled.

Since birds do not have sweat glands and since feathers are such effective insulators of heat, a hummingbird cannot cool itself by means of its skin, as man does. Instead, the bird utilizes an internal evaporative cooling system. When it is hot, the bird pants, which allows for an influx of fresh, cool air. This method of evaporative cooling is particularly important when the bird is flying, since its flight muscles create a great deal of heat as they transform stored fat into energy.

SKELETAL SYSTEM

The skeleton is the framework of the hummingbird's body. It gives shape to the bird and provides protection for its fragile yet vital internal organs. The skeleton also anchors the muscles that enable the bird to move. (The drawing of the skeletal system can be found on p. 38.)

Hummingbird bones are extremely light not only because of their diminutive size but also because most of them are not solid but porous. In fact, some of the bones, such as those of the wing and leg, are totally hollow.

The light, air-filled bone structure of the hummingbird is an adaptation that aids flight. However, these lightweight bones are themselves not fragile. On the contrary, they are actually much stronger than solid bones. The porous bones are strengthened internally by a series of struts. The air-filled interiors cushion shocks and combine with extreme flexibility to protect the bird against impacts which might otherwise severely injure it.

Basically, the skeleton of the hummingbird is similar to that of other birds. There are, however, certain structures that are of particular interest.

For example, supporting the tongue and extending behind it is the hyoid apparatus, which forms two arms (or horns) under the jaw and passes around the back of the skull. Extension of the hummingbird's unusually long tongue involves the sliding forward of these horns.

Also, more than half of the hummingbird's vertebral column is made up of cervical vertebrae. Hummingbirds have 14 or 15 cervical vertebae, depending on the species.

The hummingbird has eight pairs of ribs, two pairs more than most birds, particularly land birds. In addition, its thin, bony sternum is considered the largest, proportionately speaking, in the entire class of birds. Although some swifts display the same ratio of length to depth of keel, the hummingbird sternum is not only deep but also long, running nearly the entire length of the body. It has a rounded edge, and the ridges to which the muscles attach are quite large and prominent. This keel shape provides more space for the attachment of the flight muscles that enable the hummingbird to perform its distinctive aerial acrobatics.

The radius and ulna make up the hummingbird's tiny forearm. The swift stroke of the hummingbird's wing is due to a short humerus and forearm and extremely long hand bones that support the shafts of the large primary feathers. The inner portion of the wing is also quite short, and it has been determined that a hummingbird cannot flex its wings as can other birds. The hand bones that correspond to the second, third and fourth fingers of man's hand are extremely long.

With respect to the pectoral girdle, the coracoids of a hummingbird have a rather exceptional structure in comparison with those of other birds. While the majority of birds possess a wing-raising tendon that runs from the pectoralis minor through a notch in the coracoid's upper end, that of a hummingbird has a notch that is bridged over, and the tendon passes securely through the opening thus formed. A shallow cup-and-ball joint, formed where the coracoid joins the sternum, is a feature peculiar to swifts and hummingbirds.

The hummingbird foot has four digits, three pointing forward and one pointed backward. This last one, known as the hallux, corresponds to the big toe of man. The inner or first toe, which has two joints or phalanges, is the shortest, the second has three and the third, which is generally the longest, has four. The fourth toe has five joints. The two inner ones are slightly connected at the base. Some species of hummingbirds have very small toes with small and rounded nails, while others have long, very sharp and quite hooked nails.

SMELL

In most birds, the sense of smell is not very strong. Olfactory lobes in the avian brain are not very well developed, and the olfactory nerve endings found in nasal passages of mammals are absent in those of birds.

Flowers that have evolved to attract hummingbirds are conspicuously lacking in fragrance. Their odorlessness may have the function of discouraging competition with insects that would be drawn to fragrant blossoms, but more probably is due to the fact that plants that depend on hummingbirds for fertilization need no fragrance, since a hummingbird does not use its sense of smell to select its food source. In fact, the bird will readily feed from such mildly scented flowers as the poisonous oleander until repelled by its offensive taste.

TASTE

As a rule, birds have from 40 to 60 taste buds—many fewer than man, who has approximately 10,000. Perhaps the fact that birds swallow their food so quickly has eliminated the need for these sensory indicators.

Taste buds are located in the posterior portion of the mouth in such places as the soft palate, under the tongue in mucous membrane, at the opening into the larynx and on the salivary glands of the tongue. From a structural standpoint, those of hummingbirds are believed to be similar to those of other birds, although special follicular cells are found around the taste buds of some species.

Hummingbirds can discern the amount of sugar in solutions from which they feed and seem to prefer sweeter concentrations. This has been determined in experiments in which they have rejected solutions composed of less than 1 part sugar to 8 parts water.

TONGUE

The slim tongue of the hummingbird is a particularly unusual organ. It is extremely long, translucent and bifid, which means that it is divided into two equal lobes or parts by a median cleft.

While at rest, the tongue fits perfectly inside the lower portion of the bill. It is, however, extensile; it is forced out by the action of the os hyoids, or

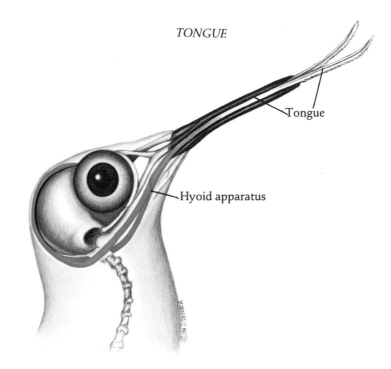

TONGUE

Tongue

Hyoid apparatus

hyoid apparatus, which are found around the posterior portion of the skull. This motion is important in enabling the bird to harvest the nectar found deep within long, tubular flowers.

Near its base, the tongue is flat, is covered by a layer of stratified epithelial tissue and bears a slight groove along the middle. Near its halfway point, it divides completely lengthwise, and each tip is pointed. Another groove is found along the outside edge. Flanges composed of membraneous tissue are located along the outside surfaces after the point where the two tubes separate.

These fimbriated, or fringed, tissues roll up inwardly to create two tubes, which may be important in consuming nectar. Since the soft feathery tongue tips are not found in all hummingbirds, it has been suggested that they are actually created by the powerful action exerted when the bird forces out its tongue.

The first scientists who studied hummingbirds believed that the tongue had a sticky surface to which insects adhered. It has been proved, however, that this is not so. Nor do the two distal divisions move in a tweezerlike motion to catch insects. The fimbriated tongue tips, however, are useful in capturing minute creatures that are sometimes found deep in the blossoms from which hummingbirds feed.

Also, until recently, scientists and hummingbird enthusiasts held to the belief that a hummingbird sucked in its liquid food through hollow chambers in its tongue. This theory has conclusively been proved false, for the tongue itself does not consist of these tubes, nor does it join with other outside tubes.

The extremely long translucent tongue of the hummingbird can extend to reach deep into tubular flowers to reach the sweet nectar within. Contrary to popular belief, the tongue does not suck the liquid up into the mouth. Instead, the bird licks nectar at a rate of about 13 licks per second. Berylline and Broad-billed hummingbirds.

It is believed, instead, that nectar is drawn into the tongue by means of capillary action and is swallowed when the bird draws it in.

The tongue collects nectar by means of a licking motion at a rate of about 13 licks per second, regardless of the size of the bird. The larger the bird and tongue, the greater amount of nectar is consumed with each lick and the greater the rate of intake. Approximately 3.1 to 7.9 grams of nectar are consumed by a hummingbird at a feeder at one time.

TOUCH

Since the majority of the hummingbird's body is covered with feathers, its sense of touch is necessarily limited to the few spots that are bare.

Its tactile senses, like those of other birds, are quite underdeveloped compared with those of mammals. Needless to say, they can feel both the ground and their perches with their feet, and when we see them scratching we can only assume that they also feel other sensations such as itching.

UROLOGICAL SYSTEM

During digestion, nonnutritive liquid wastes are separated from food that has been consumed. The urological system is the means by which these wastes are removed from the body, and in a hummingbird, as in other birds, it is composed of four basic parts—two kidneys and two ureters.

UROGENITAL SYSTEM

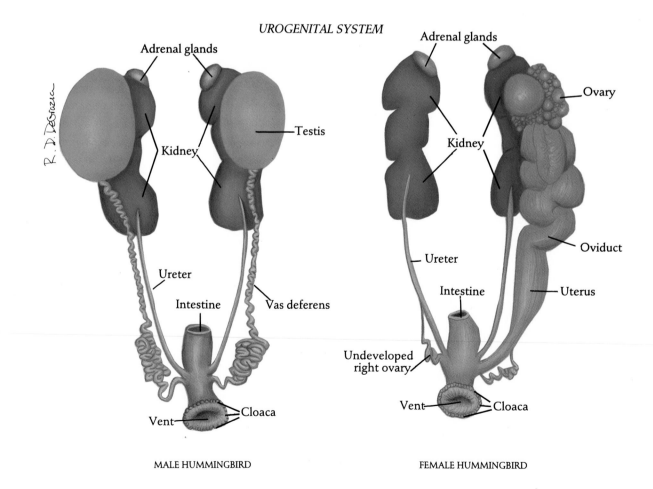

MALE HUMMINGBIRD

FEMALE HUMMINGBIRD

Waste products are carried by the bloodstream to the glandular kidneys, which are located behind the lungs in the area where the pelvic bones fuse with the synasacrum. Dark brown in color, they are composed of three lobes, each of which divides into still smaller lobes.

Within the lobes is a complex system of capsules, tubules and blood vessels that work together to filter out liquid wastes and ammonia, a harmful residue that is a by-product of protein metabolism (and that is chemically converted into uric acid before it reaches the kidney).

Urine leaves the kidneys by means of two thin ureters. Although some water is reabsorbed into the kidneys and ureters, the remainder is excreted. The narrow ureters carry it directly to the cloaca, where it is expelled immediately through the vent, the bird having no control over its expulsion. The hummingbird, like other birds, does not have a bladder; such an organ would only weigh it down. Urine mixes with indigestible solids and produces the white color of bird droppings.

In addition to their vital role in removing unnecessary fluids from the body, the kidneys are responsible for controlling the fluid levels in the body by holding in water when the bird has not consumed enough and voiding excess liquid when necessary.

VOICE

The larynx is a chamber located between the glottis and trachea or windpipe. Since there are no vocal cords located within it, it does not serve as the bird's voice box as it does in man.

Instead, the organ of voice is the syrinx, a structure located at the base of the trachea at the point where it bifurcates into the bronchi. Birds are the only animals that have this organ.

Although sound originates within two separate areas, each located within a bronchus, the exact method by which it is produced is not yet known and is a subject of great controversy. It is believed, however, that exhaled air causes the elastic tympaniform membranes of the syrinx to vibrate and thus produce sound. Other anatomical structures may be involved as well. The trachea apparently does not play a major part in producing sound.

Male Anna's with molting gorget.

Feathers

4

Of all animated beings, this [the hummingbird] is the most elegant in form and the most brilliant in colour. The stones and metals polished by art are not comparable to this gem of nature: she has placed it in the order of birds, but among the tiniest of the race. . . . The emerald, the ruby, and the topaz, glitter in its garb, which is never soiled with the dust of earth; for, leading an aerial life, it rarely touches the turf even for an instant.

George Louis Leclerc, Comte de Buffon
L'Histoire naturelle
1775

There can be no question why hummingbirds have long been referred to as "feathered jewels" and why their dwellings in zoos are called jewel rooms. Audubon called the hummingbird a "glittering fragment of the rainbow," and a cabinet of hummingbird skins was once praised as "an impressive spectacle which fills the mind not only with delight, but with deeper emotions; for in silent, but eloquent language, like the galaxy of stars in the firmament, it proclaims the divine hand of the Creator."

Their sparkling plumage has been alluded to as having "the hue of roses steeped in liquid fire," and a green dot on the hummingbird's forehead was once termed "a star brighter than Venus, the queen of planets."

Their lustrous feathers having been thus described, it should come as no surprise that a little more than a century ago, the procuring and selling of hummingbird skins was a lucrative business. French and Belgian dealers, in particular, sold them to Europeans not only for scientific purposes but also for the creation of such elegant ladies' accessories as bonnets and feather fans.

Thousands of hummingbird skins were exported annually to Europe from Santa Fé de Bogotá, Rio de Janeiro and other South American cities. One recorded consignment from a port in Brazil consisted of 3,000 skins of the Ruby-topaz Hummingbird alone. In 1888, over 12,000 skins were sold at a sale in London. In the same year, a total of 400,000 hummingbirds and other North and South American birds were also sold in London.

Further, skins of these little birds could be readily obtained from such dealers as naturalist Adolphe Boucard, who, in his monthly journal entitled

The Humming Bird, offered a wide array of specimens for prices ranging from a paltry 2 shillings to a high of 200 shillings.

The slaves of Brazilian citizens were prevailed upon to prepare hummingbird skins for sale. In addition, Indians in the Americas also discovered that providing skins was a profitable endeavor and quickly acquired the art of skinning and preserving the unfortunate creatures. Mexican convents, too, were supplied with hummingbird skins, since nuns in the New World fashioned flowers from glittering hummingbird feathers.

How were hummingbird skins obtained? The birds were best killed by shotguns with tiny no. 10 and 11 shot, since larger sizes of shot would damage the plumage and render the specimen worthless. Indians, on the other hand, demonstrated their prowess in downing hummingbirds with tiny clay balls from primitive blowpipes.

Birds are the only creatures on earth that have feathers, and every bird has them. They are very important to the creature, since they give it the streamlined shape that allows it to fly so effectively. The feather shafts are well adapted for flight, being light and hollow.

Warm-blooded animals lose heat in direct proportion to their surface area. Since the hummingbird is so small, it has a greater surface area per unit of weight than larger birds and, therefore, it is harder for it to sustain its normal body temperature. It is able to thermoregulate itself, however, since it has more feathers per unit of body surface than larger birds.

Feathers also cover the hummingbird's body and protect its thin, delicate skin. With respect to its size and weight, nothing else of comparable dimensions is as strong as a feather. It is light, strong and flexible and, if bent, will spring back.

The colors of feathers enable the bird to communicate and protect itself.

The smaller the bird, the fewer feathers it has. In 1936, the feathers of a male Ruby-throated Hummingbird were counted and the little bird was found to have 940 contour feathers; a Whistling Swan had 25,216. In 1949, 1,518 feathers were counted on a female Ruby-throated. In 1956, a total of 1,459 feathers were found on a male Allen's Hummingbird and 1,659 on a female of the same species.

In order to understand the true usefulness of the feather, it is necessary first to describe it.

The shaft of a feather has a lower portion, called the calamus or quill, and an upper portion, called the rachis. Barbs, or rami, extend outward from the rachis and adhere tightly to each other. Barbules, or radii, extend outward from the barbs and give the feather its weblike quality. There are hundreds of pairs of them per barb, and it is not unusual for there to be several hundred thousand in a feather that contains a few hundred barbs.

Barbicels, or cilia, are tiny projections that extend outward from the barbules. A good number of them have hamuli, which are minuscule hooklike projections and are visible only under a microscope. Barbicels attach to other barbicels so snugly that air cannot pass through.

Hamuli, the tiny hooks on the ends of some barbicels, are generally found only on the ends of contour feathers. This feature allows more air to be trapped in the body's many air pockets. Hamuli hook over the barbules situated above them, and this intricate construction keeps the many-barbed vane in one flexible and sturdy piece.

Except in penguins and the kiwi, feathers do not grow at random over the bodies of birds. Instead, they grow in particular regions called feather tracts or pterylae.

Pterylosis is the arrangement of contour feathers over the bird's body. There is a characteristic pattern of these feather tracts for each kind of bird. Bare portions of skin are called apteria.

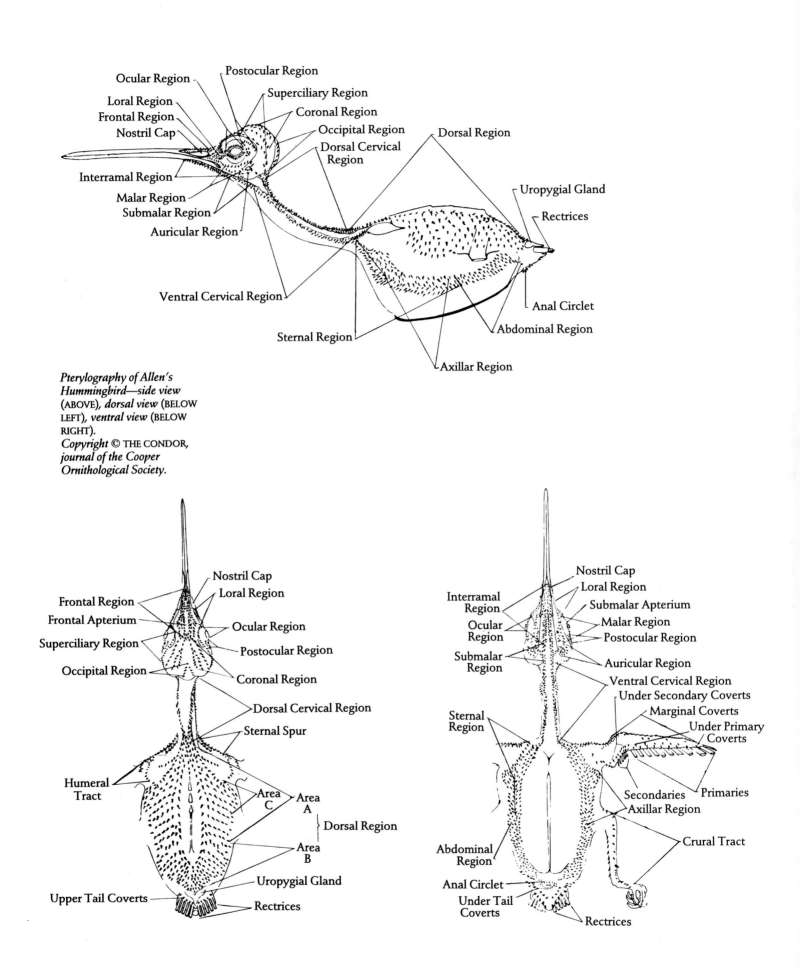

Ocular Region
Postocular Region
Loral Region
Superciliary Region
Frontal Region
Coronal Region
Nostril Cap
Occipital Region
Dorsal Cervical Region
Dorsal Region
Uropygial Gland
Rectrices
Interramal Region
Malar Region
Submalar Region
Auricular Region
Ventral Cervical Region
Anal Circlet
Abdominal Region
Sternal Region
Axillar Region

Pterylography of Allen's Hummingbird—side view (ABOVE), *dorsal view* (BELOW LEFT), *ventral view* (BELOW RIGHT).
Copyright © THE CONDOR, *journal of the Cooper Ornithological Society.*

Nostril Cap
Loral Region
Frontal Region
Frontal Apterium
Ocular Region
Superciliary Region
Postocular Region
Occipital Region
Coronal Region
Dorsal Cervical Region
Sternal Spur
Humeral Tract
Area C
Area A
Dorsal Region
Area B
Upper Tail Coverts
Uropygial Gland
Rectrices

Nostril Cap
Loral Region
Interramal Region
Submalar Apterium
Ocular Region
Malar Region
Postocular Region
Submalar Region
Auricular Region
Ventral Cervical Region
Under Secondary Coverts
Marginal Coverts
Under Primary Coverts
Sternal Region
Secondaries
Primaries
Axillar Region
Crural Tract
Abdominal Region
Anal Circlet
Under Tail Coverts
Rectrices

Hummingbirds have few or no downy feathers in apteria. These bare portions, however, are not evident, since they are covered by feathers that have grown in the feather tracts. There are usually eight tracts.

Down feathers are also known as neossoptiles. Since a down feather has no upper shaft, its barbs extend from the quill, do not have any hooks and therefore do not make up a vane. Instead, they weave together to create an insulated area filled with air.

Hummingbirds are altricial birds, which means that they are born with little or no down covering and are raised by their mothers in the nest. Within the time frame of a few days to a few weeks, the nestling acquires its new coat of feathers.

Some natal down is evident on nestlings of most species of hummingbirds. In the center portion of the spinal tract of the Ruby-throated Hummingbird, for example, are 12 pairs of beige neossoptiles arranged in longitudinal rows.

These feathers are generally long and filamentous. Twenty-five species of hummingbirds have been noted to have 8 to 12 pairs of these downy feathers. An exception is the Rufous-breasted Hermit, whose nestlings were found to have approximately 25–76 downy-type filaments distributed on eight or nine tracts. These neossoptiles were thought to be stouter than those of other hummingbirds, but further investigation revealed that they were actually closely packed and covered by an almost transparent sheathlike covering. Further, they were shorter and had barbules, which are usually absent in natal down.

This photograph of an abandoned Allen's nestling shows the long downy feathers arranged in longitudinal rows present in many hummingbird chicks at birth. South Coast Botanic Gardens, Palos Verdes, California.

The nestling's juvenal plumage appears soon after hatching.

It appears that some species of hummingbirds lack downy coverings altogether or have it arranged differently. Down has been found on the capital tract in the Glittering-throated Emerald and in the Ruby-topaz Hummingbird. It has been suggested, however, that these coronal filaments were mistakenly identified and that in fact they are from the dorsal region. Juvenal plumage begins to appear soon after hatching.

Contour feathers are the flight feathers and visible feathers of the body. They cover the bird's body, wings and tail and have vanes and well-developed shafts. Collectively, they give the bird its streamlined form. The longest feathers are those of the wing and tail.

The remiges, or flight feathers, are the most highly developed feathers. There are two kinds—primaries and secondaries. Primaries are very specialized feathers and are counted from the inside outward. Secondaries are numbered from the outermost inward.

The number of secondaries seems to be contingent upon the size of the wing bones. Since hummingbird wings are quite short, there are only six or seven secondaries compared to the nine or ten found in most passerine birds.

The bones of the hummingbird hand are extremely long and are the base for the primary feathers, which are also elongated. The primary feathers of most hummingbirds are generally longer as they near the wing tip, with the longest one being that of the wing tip itself.

Hummingbirds, such as the Broad-tailed, that have specialized wing tips for purposes of creating sound have shorter outer primaries than other spe-

Anna's Hummingbird showing
remiges (primaries and secondaries)
and rectrices.

cies. The outermost primary of the Streamertail, however, whose wings are not specially designed for sound production, is shorter than the one next to it, but this is an exception.

There are fewer secondaries than primaries, and they are shorter. There are usually six of them, but an underdeveloped seventh is evident in some species, such as the Allen's.

The rectrices are the bird's tail feathers. Although sometimes the rectrices are referred to collectively as the tail, the actual tail is the muscular portion of the bird's body known as the pygostyle or "pope's nose."

With the exception of the remiges, the rectrices are the most specialized of all bird's feathers. They are important for braking, steering and balance.

Hummingbirds have ten tail feathers, except for a few species such as the Spatule-tail Hummingbird. The rectrices of this bird are four in number, with two being very highly developed. The innermost rectrices of the Anna's and Costa's are substantially wider than those on the outer edges of the tail. There are notched feathers located in the tail of the Rufous Hummingbird (next to the middle pair), and it has been theorized that they may mechanically produce sound.

Tails can be forked, wedge-shaped, graduated, rounded on both sides, embellished with streamers or even more variated. The tails of the Broad-billed, Lucifer, Ruby-throated and Buff-bellied hummingbirds are forked.

There are two kinds of colors—those caused by pigments and those caused by feather structure. The red-brown color of the Rufous, for example, is the result of pigment, as are the various other browns and dusky blacks sometimes found in a hummingbird's plumage. There is no red or yellow in their plumage.

Structural colors, on the other hand, may be caused by refraction or interference. Refraction coloration is what transforms daylight to strips of colored light as it passes through a prism. Interference coloration is what produces the visible hues in thin films such as soap bubbles and oil slicks.

Early naturalists were fascinated by the jewellike plumage of hummingbirds but were unable to explain its unique fiery glow. They theorized that it

Wing tips of the Broad-tailed's outer primaries are slightly forked to produce a sound unique to this species.

The reddish-brown color of the Rufous is the result of pigmented color.

must have something to do with the structure of the feathers and the reflection of light upon them. One, René-Primevére Lesson, noted that the feathers appeared to have "myriads of little facets, so disposed as to present so many angles to the incidence of light which will be diversely reflected, according to the position of the feather"—an observation which, while not entirely correct, was at least on the right track.

Some early scientists, on the other hand, erred in their belief that the iridescent color was caused by certain materials contained in the bloodstream of these tiny birds and that their colors were enhanced as blood circulated throughout the body.

Closer observation determined that the glittering feathers were composed of barbules that were cylindrical in form and had a concave shape. It was surmised that light hitting them from a horizontal angle reflected a gem-like color, and light from a vertical direction would be absorbed and result in black or a total absence of color.

Isaac Newton speculated that thin laminates, or plates, might be the cause of iridescence in insects and birds, but early microscopes were not powerful enough to detect these multilayered films. In 1857, it was first suggested that iridescence was produced by interference.

We now know that only the top third of each feather is iridescent and that its barbules do not have barbicels or hamuli. Instead, barbules of iridescent hummingbird feathers have minute elliptical structures of varying sizes called platelets. They resemble a mosaic-tile floor with dark spaces in between.

Feathers from the gorgets of the Black-chinned, Costa's, Bluethroated and Anna's hummingbirds. Notice that only the top third is iridescent.

These colored granules have air bubbles contained within them. The thickness of the platelet itself and the amount of air inside determines the specific color seen.

The feathers of the gorget and crown are among the most specialized. Their barbules resemble flat mirrors, and light that hits them can be reflected in only one direction. The sun, viewer and bird must be aligned properly to behold the sparkling plumage at its best. This is why from a different angle the color seen may be dusky green, violet or even red. When no light shines on them they appear black.

Barbules of the back feathers are curved inward to resemble concave mirrors. This distinctive shape allows light shining on them to be reflected in all directions. For this reason, a hummingbird's back (such as the Anna's) is always seen as a golden green that is less intense.

Iridescent coloration is evident on almost all of the rest of the bird, with the exception of the primaries, secondaries and, in some cases, tail feathers. Thus, the important feathers of flight are spared the weak-vaned structure of iridescent feathers.

It has never been determined that the sparkling plumage of hummingbirds is used for any purpose other than ornamentation. Indeed, the dazzling colors of the male play an important role in courtship display.

From time to time we hear of albino hummingbirds. These birds, whose white plumage may have a rosy or brownish cast, usually have a short life span, since they often have defects in both organ systems and physiology. In North America, there have been reports of both Black-chinned and Allen's albino hummingbirds.

Molting is the periodic replacement of feathers that have become broken or worn from abrasion. Each species of hummingbird, like other birds, has a particular pattern of molt. Most birds molt gradually, for if feathers were dropped from one entire area at once, there would be severe problems in insulation and flight. The molting process thus never deprives the bird of its powerful flight ability or the protection of its feathery coat.

ANNA'S HUMMINGBIRD
These two views of a male Anna's clearly depict the iridescent quality of its crown and gorget. The brilliant helmet glows completely when seen head-on, but parts of it go dark when the bird turns away.

The iridescent feathers of the back are constructed so as to reflect light evenly in all directions, as seen in this photograph of a male White-eared.

When feathers are broken or otherwise lost, they are immediately replaced so as to not interfere with the bird's ability to fly. Male Broad-billed.

69

While in the molting cycle, a hummingbird may slack off from its usual fast pace, for the process of feather replacement takes a great deal of energy and affects the bird's metabolism.

Molt in hummingbirds begins with the loss of the first primary; each succeeding outermost primary is then molted until the eighth is lost. The loss of the eighth is followed by the nonsequential molting of the tenth and then the ninth primaries.

When the outer primaries are lost, the hummingbird's power requirements are increased, and it has been theorized that the pattern of molt of the tenth and then the ninth primaries probably reduces the impact of the bird's losing its feathers.

BLUE-THROATED HUMMINGBIRD
In this photograph, the sheath of the completely grown tenth primary is being shed as the ninth is just coming in. Note also the pinfeathers of the wing coverts and gorget.

A handful of pinfeathers appear on the bird's head.

One week later, many more have broken through, replacing those that have dropped.

When the flight feathers have almost fully grown in, the rectrices are shed. The Red-billed Azurecrown, however, apparently loses its two inner tail feathers before its flight feathers.

With respect to the secondaries, the feathers are lost from both sides simultaneously. Rectrices either start at both outer ends or from the inner feathers outward.

MALE BLACK-CHINNED HUMMINGBIRD
Immature Black-chinned Hummingbird with iridescent violet spot on throat.

Acquiring its adult plumage. Ragged crown contrasts sharply with fresh violet gorget feathers.

Its distinctive purple band becomes more and more visible. This bird's ninth (and last to molt) primary can also be seen pushing outward. Clumps of gray feathers on the chin dangled dangerously while this picture was being taken and looked as if they would fall at the slightest movement.

The molting process completed, this Black-chinned poses for a portrait in his brand-new adult plumage.

MALE BROAD-BILLED HUMMINGBIRD
Just prior to molting, this Broad-billed's tail feathers appear ragged.

In the process of acquiring a new tail. Also note molting primaries, gorget, wing coverts.

Immature bird acquiring adult plumage. Note pinfeathers on tail, primaries, wing coverts and crown.

The breeding season of the Anna's Hummingbird is from December to June. When these birds start their molt in late May, they cease their combative, territorial behavior and can even sometimes be observed feeding harmoniously from the same feeder. It has even been noted that they appear to gain considerable weight during this time, probably a direct result of decreased activity.

The Anna's molt ends around the late part of August or early September, and it is at this time that the birds resume their territorial hostilities. Most males have attained their full plumage by late November and early December.

The molt of the female Anna's Hummingbird is shorter and lasts from June to October.

The molt of the adult male Anna's begins in the alar tract when the first and second primaries are shed. The rest of the body begins to molt only after the flight feathers have almost finished molting.

Feathers of the ventral and spinal tracts grow in at roughly the same rate, and those of the latter may actually finish their molt sooner.

ANNA'S HUMMINGBIRD
Molting male Anna's
Hummingbird.

Feathers of the crown and gorget start to drop and are quickly replaced with pinfeathers encased in white sheaths. Notice uncovered ear cavity below the eye.

One week later, the Anna's looks shabby and grotesque.

Normally handsome, the bird goes through a brief period of unsightliness.

*Newly refurbished, the male is now
ready to begin courting.*

When the first five or six new primaries have grown in, the tail begins its molt. The two inner pairs of rectrices drop, and there may be a slight interval before the remaining feathers are shed. In fact, the first rectrices to molt are often partially or fully grown before the rest of the tail resumes its molt.

The iridescent feathers of the head and gorget molt last. They are replaced toward the end of the molting cycle and quite near to the beginning of the breeding season. These feathered areas play a very important part in courtship display, and it is appropriate that they are in the strongest and most beautiful condition for the breeding season. It has been suggested that male hummingbirds will not even engage in courtship display until their gorgets are completely replaced.

It takes from 10 to 15 days for a male Anna's Hummingbird to acquire a new gorget.

ALLEN'S HUMMINGBIRD
With only a few more gorget pinfeathers left to burst open, this Allen's male is nearing the end of its annual molt.

Feather ruffling helps break apart white pinfeather sheaths.

COSTA'S HUMMINGBIRD
The immature male Costa's is often mistakenly identified as a Lucifer.

Male Costa's five days after acquiring its amethyst helmet. It will continue to glow dully for several more days before attaining its brilliant shine.

WHITE-EARED HUMMINGBIRD
Immature male White-eared.

Adult White-eared.

**BROAD-BILLED
HUMMINGBIRD**
*Immature male Broad-billed feeds
from Scarlet Bouvardia*
(BOUVARDIA TERNIFOLIA).

*Ragged immature male Broad-billed
just before molting.*

RUFOUS HUMMINGBIRD
Immature male Rufous showing
brilliant speck of copper on gorget.

Adult male Rufous feeding from
Scarlet Penstemon (PENSTEMON
LABROSUS).

Momentarily satisfied after a drink from these LOESELIA MEXICANA *blossoms, a male White-eared, having backed away, makes a turn to his left.*

Flight

$\Big|\,5$

The hummingbird is nature's helicopter.

John Zugschwert
Executive Director
American Helicopter Society
1983

The incomparable aerial acrobatics of the hummingbird have long fascinated those who have observed it, from the native Indians who inhabited the great primeval forests of the Americas, to the first Europeans who described them in the sixteenth century, to Americans today who see them migrating through their backyards every year.

Hummingbirds' flight abilities are clearly superior to those of any other bird, for in addition to flying forward, hummingbirds can propel themselves backward or to the right or left, hover motionless and even fly upside down. In fact, the only aerial maneuver they are incapable of is soaring.

In order to be able to truly appreciate the hummingbird's vast powers of flight, however, one should understand something of bird flight in general.

A bird, which can flex its wings at joints in the wrist, elbow and shoulder, flies by means of flapping flight. With its body in a horizontal position, the bird moves its wings forward in a downward arc that subsequently flows into an upward stroke. Upon lowering its wing, the bird is propelled forward and upward. A propeller-type action, which moves the bird swiftly forward while requiring minimal effort, is provided during both the up and down strokes by the hand. In the meantime, lift and stability are furnished by the secondary feathers located at the base of the wing, while the tip of the wing provides thrust.

The shape of the bird's wing, convex above and concave below, generates lift from different velocities of airflow over its upper and lower surfaces.

During the upward stroke, or recovery stroke as it is sometimes called,

*Immature male Rufous feeding from Scarlet Penstemon (*PENSTEMON BRIDGESII). *The hummingbird is the only bird that can hover and fly forward, backward, to the right or left and upside down.*

little power is required. Should the bird encounter any air turbulence or resistance, it can be decreased by a movement of the primary feathers called slotting. During slotting, both the alular quills and the primaries, which have thinner outer vanes, spread apart to form slots through which air passes.

In addition, both wings and feathers are capable of individually moving to compensate for any kind of air current or wing condition a bird may encounter while airborne.

The movement of the wings is controlled by the bird's pectorals, or breast muscles. The hummingbird's unusually strong flight capability is evidenced anatomically by the fact that these specialized muscles account for approximately 25–30 percent of its total weight, compared to 15–25 percent in other skillful fliers, 6–7 percent in a chicken and about 5 percent in man.

In the flight of other birds, too, the upstroke is not as important a factor as the downstroke, as demonstrated by the fact that the muscles governing this upward movement weigh only 5–10 percent of what the downstroke muscles weigh. In the hummingbird, however, the upstroke is nearly equal in importance to the downstroke, and the upstroke muscles are tremendous, weighing fully 50 percent of the weight of the downstroke muscles.

Unlike those of birds that hop or run about, the tiny feet of most species of hummingbirds are really quite useless except for perching. Indeed, some people mistakenly think that they have no feet at all! Consequently, they depend upon their flight to get them from one place to another, even when the distance is only a few inches.

It may be surprising to learn that although the hummingbird is considered to be one of the avian world's strongest fliers, its method of flying is one of the least efficient. The truth is that the size and shape of the hummingbird's wing is suited only for a mode of flight that depends upon a great deal of energy expenditure. On the other hand, the wing is of the perfect dimension for a bird of its light weight and diminutive size and allows the creature to control and maneuver itself very well in the air. In fact, its high-speed wing and characteristic whirring flight are perfectly designed for rapid flying in the open areas in which it exists.

The hummingbird's small, stiff wing is tapered and narrow, with an upper surface that is less convex than in other birds. In addition, the heaviest portion of the wing is situated close to the base of the bird's body. Both the stout humerus and the radius and ulna are very short, and this compact little arm moves freely only at the bird's remarkably flexible shoulder joint. It is at this joint that the wing rotates almost 180 degrees to enable the bird to fly in its distinctive way. In fact, the oarlike wing movement is the direct result of the lack of flexibility of the wrist and elbow joints.

Because of the very short length of the hummingbird's arm, it can easily be seen that the bird's wing is made up almost completely of an extremely long hand, thereby proving the curious fact that the hummingbird, like the swift, flies with its hands.

The primary feathers of the hummingbird do not separate to form slots like those of other birds, probably due to both their exceedingly narrow vanes (which measure $\frac{1}{10}$ inch in a Ruby-throated Hummingbird) and their stout quills. In addition, the alula is either very small or completely missing, but this is not surprising in a bird that hovers and has a very strong and rapid upstroke.

Although cinematic pictures of birds on the wing revealed a lot of new information about bird flight, those of hummingbirds did not. Instead, it took the invention of the stroboscope to unravel the mysteries of how they fly. Motion pictures made from a camera connected to a stroboscope with a flash duration of 1/100,000 second finally allowed the bird's unusual method of flying to be studied properly.

It was discovered that the little bird actually begins its flight prior to leaving its perch. For example, one hummingbird was observed to lift itself off a twig after three wing strokes which took place in 7/1,000 second. Also, when the bird starts to fly, it has already almost reached top speed. In addition, it is interesting to note that the hummingbird rises into the air entirely on its own power and does not use the twig or branch from which it lifts off as a brace to push against when taking to the air.

These two photographs of a male Ruby-throated show how a hummingbird begins flying before leaving its perch. Thus, when airborne, it has already reached top speed.

90   *Male Allen's starting his flight from
a sitting position.*

Hummingbirds use flapping flight to propel themselves forward, but in contrast to other birds the power of the downstroke and upstroke is almost equal. Note the tiny, almost useless feet. Broad-tailed.

A hummingbird flies forward by means of flapping flight, and its wings, which remain rigid, trace a nearly vertical oval in the air. Both upstrokes and downstrokes are important in propelling the bird forward and upward, although it has been suggested that the downward portion may be more important. In the flapping flight of other birds, downstroke generates much more power than the upstroke, but both are about equal in the hummingbird.

When the bird is flying slowly forward, the tips of the wings trace another oval shape, this one tilted or slanted so that the upper end is to the rear of the bird and the lower portion is to the front of the bird.

With all due respect to the Duke of Argyle, hummingbirds, like insects, *can* fly backward. The bird can quickly change gears, so to speak, from forward flight to rise backward by merely slanting the angle of its wings. When flying backward, its body is in a nearly vertical plane, its tail is tilted and its wings trace an almost horizontal circle above its body. Its wings also beat slightly faster during this kind of flight, although the speed attained is not rapid.

Hummingbirds are the only birds that can fly backward. Here a male Anna's backs away from a patch of California Fuchsia (ZAUSCHNERIA CALIFORNIA).

When frightened suddenly, a hummingbird can make a fast getaway by flying upside down, a feat it accomplishes by spreading its tail and using it to lead its body into a backward somersault. After reversing its wing beat to propel it a little ways (its head is down and its feet are up), it will then turn over again and continue its flight in normal fashion.

Hummingbirds are probably best known for their ability to hover motionless in the air while feeding. Of all the different kinds of animal movement, this method of aerial suspension requires the most energy, for it

This Calliope Hummingbird backs away from the Scarlet Penstemon (PENSTEMON LABROSUS) *and starts rolling to the left.*

demands that the wings move unceasingly. It is believed that because hovering consumes so much of the hummingbird's energy, this mode of flight evolved for feeding purposes rather than for locomotion.

There are several other birds that, to the casual observer, may seem to hover. These include the Black-shouldered Kite, the American Kestrel, the Belted Kingfisher and Leach's Storm Petrel. However, theirs is not a true hovering flight and cannot be sustained for very long.

It was thought at one time that a bird could hover only when there was

The stiff, powerful wing of the hummingbird traces a figure eight in the air while hovering. White-eared, feeding on LOESELIA MEXICANA.

sufficient wind passing under its wings to provide lift, but this was proved to be false when it was observed that a hummingbird could hover successfully in a totally enclosed space.

When a hummingbird hovers, its body is in a vertical position and its fully extended wings do not flap up and down. Instead, they move forward and backward in a figure-eight pattern that is parallel to the ground. During the forward and back strokes the wings make two almost-180-degree turns. During the forward stroke the wing pushes the air downward, and during the backward strokes it pushes the air upward. As in forward flying, the upstroke is almost equal to the downstroke.

Like a helicopter, a hummingbird can either move forward during hovering by slanting its wings forward and downward or move backward by slanting them up and back. It is also easy for a hummingbird to change its flight from stationary hovering to fast forward. In addition, it is one of the few birds that can lift itself straight up into the air, a maneuver that is useful to females who need to turn completely around in their nests.

Another example of a hovering hummingbird, this time an Anna's, feeding from the Gooseberry (RIBES SPECIOSUM).

A hummingbird can fly at top speed and yet stop suddenly and land very lightly, since even during its fastest flight it creates a very small amount of momentum.

Early observers of hummingbirds once believed that their wings beat 200 times per second when hovering. Their early experiments to determine the bird's wing rate called for a string on a violin to be tuned to match the sound the hummingbird's wings made in flight. However, the vibration rate of the violin's string was found to be excessive. This was later explained by the fact

Like a helicopter, a hummingbird can lift itself straight into the air. This Black-chinned rose from a clump of Castilleja.

that the audible tone created by the bird's wings was actually an overtone, not the fundamental tone, which was too low to be heard and would indicate a much lower vibration rate.

Birds with small or short wings beat them faster during flapping flight than larger birds. This is because the smaller the area of the wings in proportion to the weight of the bird, the greater the number of times the wings must beat to keep the bird airborne. (One downward and one upward stroke of a hovering hummingbird are considered to be one beat.)

For example, large hummingbirds with wings measuring (from wrist to

This Magnificent Hummingbird demonstrates how, after flying at top speed, it can stop suddenly and land lightly because of the small amount of momentum it creates.

wing tip) 65–88 millimeters beat them an average of 18–28 times per second. Small hummingbirds, on the other hand, with wings measuring 33–54 millimeters, beat them 38–78 times per second. Compare this to a crow, whose wing measures 325 millimeters and whose wings beat 3.6 times per second, or to a vulture, which flaps its wings once every second!

Another surprising fact is that the rate of the hummingbird's wing beats is actually *slower* than that of some other larger-winged and heavier birds. The Mockingbird, for example, beats its wings approximately 14 times per second, whereas the Giant Hummingbird, which is smaller than the Mocking-

A female Costa's retreating from an Ocotillo (FOUQUIERIA SPLENDENS). Her wings beat approximately 58 times per second.

bird, beats its wings about 8–10 times per second. This is because the wing beat of the hummingbird is a more efficient one, since power is generated on both the upstroke and the downstroke.

Wing rates of approximately 20–25 times per second seem to be the norm for hummingbirds weighing 5–7 grams. And smaller hummingbirds, like the Rufous and Ruby-throated, have been noted to have wing beats of up to 200 times per second during their nuptial dives.

It is thought that birds, no matter what their size, may have wing beats that are constant regardless of their mode of flight. The wing beats of a female Ruby-throated Hummingbird, for example, were found to remain more or less the same regardless of her aerial maneuvers. Thus, whether flying rapidly forward, backward, or hovering, her wing-beat rate did not vary more than 5 percent from 52 times per second.

Not surprisingly, some individuals, in observing the extremely rapid wing beat and swift darting flight of the hummingbird, have concluded that it is the fastest bird in the world. However, this is not the case.

The Duck Hawk probably holds that distinction, since it has been clocked at 160–180 mph. Swifts have been clocked at 100 mph, and a rate of 20–35 mph seems to be the norm for most songbirds. The maximum for such insects as wasps and bees seems to be 10 mph or a little more.

In 1937, a Ruby-throated Hummingbird was found to fly 55 mph while another was recorded at 45 mph. Also, two Blue-throated or Long-tailed Sylphs that were being kept in captivity were clocked at speeds from 30 to 47 mph with a rate that averaged 38.4 mph. A male Violet-ear was clocked at 56 mph, and there are reports of other hummingbirds in South America that fly at speeds ranging from 14 to 25 mph.

After rising approximately 50 feet into the sky, an Allen's Hummingbird, performing its nuptial dive, appeared to travel, in approximately a second, about 60 feet. An experiment with motion-picture film revealed that it attained speeds of 34, 39 and 45 mph during this courtship display.

Meanwhile, by utilizing the more sophisticated and probably more scientifically correct method of a wind tunnel, a female Ruby-throated Hummingbird was clocked at 27 mph. Its tail, which is longer than its bill, works in a rudderlike fashion to steer the bird during flight.

It is astonishing to consider the diverse aerial accomplishments of a little hummingbird, and there can be no doubt that it reigns supreme over all the other birds in the world and truly deserves to be called the champion of flight.

*Protective female Anna's with
nestful of fledglings. Note feathers
recently lost from her crown. Rancho
Santa Ana Botanical Gardens,
Claremont, California.*

Courtship and Nesting | 6

I saw one of these Nests made of Cotton-Wool, in form and bigness of the Thumb of a Man's Glove, with the Taper end sot downwards, wherein were two Eggs of the bigness of a Pea, of oval Form. Who can but admire to see the whole Body, and all the parts of a Bird folded up in an Egg, little bigger than a Pepper-Corn?

Nehemiah Grew, M.D.
Philosophical Transactions
1693

The physician Nehemiah Grew penned these charming words in an attempt to describe to his friends the picturesque nest of a hummingbird. But little more than forty years before, in 1651, it was written in the *Penny Cyclopaedia* that "while the more sober believed that they were hatched from eggs, like other birds, others fancied that they were transformed from flies, some going so far as to declare that they had been seen in the half-fly half-bird state."

Many other misconceptions have surrounded the breeding behavior of the hummingbird, despite the evidence of careful observers such as Dr. Grew. Today, more than 300 years later, it is possible to describe the hummingbird's true reproductive behavior in some detail.

The breeding period for most North American hummingbirds occurs during the spring and summer months, with the exception of the Anna's, which breeds principally during the winter and early spring. During these months, female hummers are best able to rear nestfuls of chicks with the abundance of blossoms and insects that prevail after the rainy season.

The size of a bird's sexual organs is indicative of its reproductive status and is controlled by the ductless glands. During the mating season these organs enlarge considerably, sometimes to the point where they are visible as a slight bulge in the bird's abdomen. Following the reproductive season, the gonads enter a dormant state of several months' duration, called the refractory period, which prevents the bird from attempting to breed prematurely.

At the beginning of the breeding season, male hummingbirds, many of whom have migrated hundreds of miles, arrive at their breeding grounds and choose territories. A hummingbird's criteria for making its selection is not believed to be, as with other birds, to ensure adequate food for the nesting female, although an excess of flowers does enhance mating success. Rather, the male picks a territory mindful of its food supply as it relates to him first and for mating purposes only secondarily. The exceptions to this rule are the species that mate in leks, or special courtship areas.

DISPLAY

Courtship, which refers to the actions and behavior of birds prior to (and sometimes continuing through) breeding, is an important behavior pattern, since one sex is usually more reluctant than the other to mate.

Among hummingbirds, courtship behavior consists of song, exhibition of iridescent plumage and dazzling aerial flights. In addition, these same signals are used to make other males aware of the hummingbird's dominion over a particular area.

Indeed, when a male hummingbird has chosen its territory, he becomes very belligerent and will aggressively defend his region against any intruder. This very hostile conduct, known as agonistic behavior, is thought to be the result of hormonal secretions.

Males will fight not only rival males but also birds of other species. Although they sometimes resort to physical combat to keep intruders from invading their territories, it is believed that males actually fight *less* than they would if they did not have displays. In other words, displays serve as warnings that are often heeded.

Male hummingbirds are polygynous, which means that they often mate with two or more females. Nor do they demand that the female with whom they mate be of the same species, as evidenced by the abundance of hard-to-identify hybrids.

Nevertheless, it is the *female* who seeks out the male. In fact, it is highly unlikely that a male would ever think of looking for a female.

The enterprising female hummingbird begins making her nest and, when it is nearly completed, will select a mate on the basis of either the abundance of food in his territory or his display. The male, upon seeing her for the first time, may display aggressive behavior toward her, but when she reacts in a singularly nonmale fashion he will proceed to court her. At this point, with her breeding site chosen and her nest in readiness or near readiness, the female may deign to allow the male to chase her to it.

Hummingbird courtship is a twofold process. First, the male must persuade the female not to fly out of his territory but instead to stay put and permit him to mate with her. He accomplishes this by displays that show off his shimmering feathers and fill the air with captivating (to her, at least) sounds produced either vocally or by feathery vibrations.

The second phase is that of courtship itself. During this stage hummingbirds engage in a distinctive type of acrobatic flight that varies with each species. These aerial displays, too, are often accompanied by specific vocalizations and mechanical sounds.

Display flights of North American hummingbirds are characterized by a fascinating series of aerial dives. Although once thought to be for purposes of courtship alone, they are now believed to be performed primarily for the purpose of protecting a territory against other males and only secondarily for mating. In fact, hummingbirds may engage in these flights for breeding purposes only during the earliest stages of courtship. They sometimes also perform display flights in an attempt to frighten away humans.

These acrobatic displays involve aerial climbs, dives and swoops that are executed so as to exhibit the bird's glittering plumage. Indeed, careful observation has shown that the hummingbird actually orients its dive so that its body is facing the sun, thus allowing its iridescent feathers to glitter and sparkle to best advantage. Further, it has been determined that the displays of the Anna's Hummingbirds are not often undertaken during days that are cloudy and sunless, since neither the shimmering metallic colors of its crown nor its gorget will flash and produce the desired dazzling effect. When dives are undertaken during such dreary days, they are oriented at random.

Often performed in the center of the male's territory, the displays of North American hummingbirds vary from narrow to wide arcs in the sky. Narrow arcs are favored by the Anna's, Costa's and Allen's hummingbirds, while those of the Ruby-throated are wider.

Additionally, the displays of the Costa's, Allen's, Rufous, Calliope, Anna's, Black-chinned, Ruby-throated and Broad-tailed hummingbirds are performed individually, although a joint display by two individuals of the latter species was once recorded.

Among the North American species, the display of the Anna's is probably the best known and most distinctive. With bill pointed downward, the male surges above the female or other object of display to heights ranging from 75 to 150 feet. He may sing briefly at the top of the dive, stop momentarily and then climb still higher, all the while still peering down. Finally, he will dive almost straight down at top speed and swoop dramatically over the display object. At that precise moment he emits a loud metallic popping sound while his iridescent splendor mesmerizes or frightens the object of his affection or rancor.

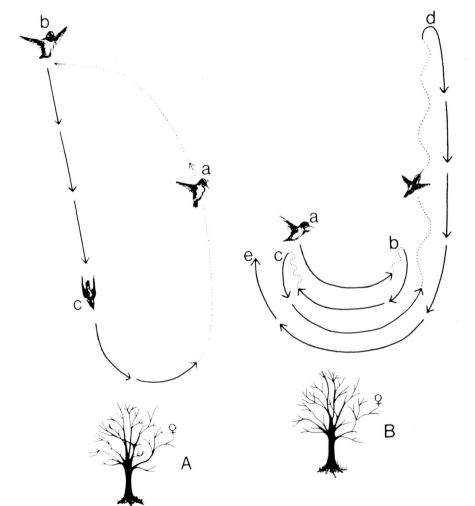

Displays of the Anna's and Allen's hummingbirds. Copyright © The Wilson Bulletin, The Wilson Ornithological Society.

As a rule, the Anna's Hummingbird performs three to eight consecutive dives, although some have been known to do as few as one and as many as a dozen or more at a time.

The shrill, explosive sound produced by the Anna's as it reaches the bottom of the dive is very loud and can be heard several hundred feet away. Its source has been the subject of great speculation. While some believed that the noise emanated from the syrinx or voice box, today the prevailing belief is that the sound is created by the bird's tail feathers.

The Allen's male flies in arcs of 20–30 feet above the female. With outspread tail, he quivers at the far edge of each arc. This flight pattern may be repeated several times, after which he will wind his way slowly upward with his bill pointed toward the sky. Once at the top, he will instantly dive down, to the accompaniment of a trill that is produced by his modified primary feathers. This display may also be repeated several times.

In addition to the extraordinary aerial dive of hummingbirds, some also perform another, little-known display sometimes referred to as shuttle flight. All hummingbirds of the genera *Stellula, Selasphorus, Calypte* and *Archilochus* use this type of display in their courtship.

Of these two displays, the shuttle is considered to be the more significant for mating. Indeed, courtship among North American hummingbirds seems to center around this series of short flights, which are performed for the benefit of the female seated either in front of or below the male.

During the shuttle flight, which usually takes place in an area of heavy undergrowth, the male swings back and forth several times. To this basic movement, each species adds its own special sound, some by vibrating specially modified feathers and others, such as those of the *Calypte* genus, vocally. A sexual chase and copulation usually follow these unusual displays.

Many species of hummingbirds also perform group courtship displays in areas called leks or arenas. These birds select their joint territory solely for the purpose of attracting females with which to mate, although within this region each male defends his own particular domain. Since the songs of these

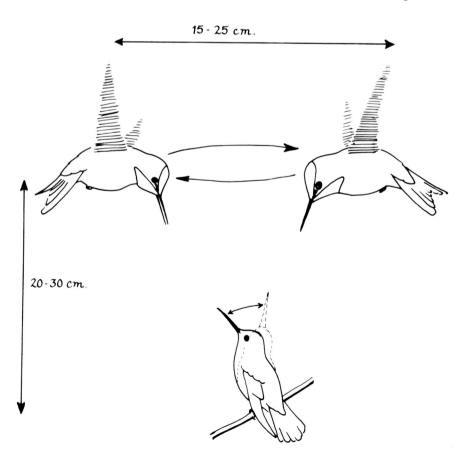

*The shuttle display of Anna's Hummingbird (*CALYPTE ANNA*). From F. G. Stiles, Copyright © 1982. Condor 84:208–25.*

hummingbirds have very short ranges, the birds sing together in what are known as courtship assemblies.

These unusual songs attract females, who visit the lek to seek males with which to mate. There often follows a sexual flight during which the female, chased by the male, will eventually submit to copulation. Both the males and females of leks may mate with more than one partner.

Species that form leks include those belonging to the genera *Phaethornis, Eutoxeres* and *Threnetes.* Blue-throated, White-eared and Berylline hummingbirds are the only North American species that mate in these peculiar arenas, which can be used over and over again.

Accurate visible accounts of mating among hummingbirds are rare, perhaps because they so often take place in areas that are difficult to reach. In fact, some experts feel that many instances of aggressive behavior between the sexes have mistakenly been termed copulation. In the opinion of other ornithologists, courtship does not exist at all for some species and the male simply overpowers the female into coition.

Nonetheless, copulation probably takes three to five seconds and occurs with the male mounting the back of the perched female, sometimes holding on to her by seizing the feathers on her head with his beak.

The egg, which forms inside the female, takes about 24 hours to develop, and sperm that passes to the oviduct during coitus fertilizes it.

Pair relationship, or the formation of pairs prior to copulation, varies greatly among other birds. But among nearly all North American hummingbirds this bond apparently lasts only as long as it takes to mate. Therefore, the role of the male hummingbird in breeding apparently does not go beyond supplying sperm and hereditary traits to female and offspring. Like sandpipers, male hummingbirds mate but leave all of the brooding, nesting and rearing of the young to the female.

Even though there have been a handful of cases in which males have been observed both incubating eggs and feeding chicks, these reports are highly doubtful, since malelike plumage has been reported in a variety of female hummingbirds (whose sex was determined by dissection) and is even a regular occurrence in some species. Further, in no case was the supposed male collected or marked and its sex verified. Reliable accounts do exist, though, of male Anna's, Sword-billed and Violet-eared hummingbirds that were seen guarding nests.

NESTS

It was actually believed during the 1800s that in order to locate a hummingbird nest all one had to do was attach a string to a hat and flutter it about. This movement would catch the attention of the male hummer, who, after swooping down on the invader, would make an easy-to-follow beeline for the nest.

This bit of amusing nonsense notwithstanding, it is understandable why someone would go to great lengths to find a hummingbird's nest, because they rank among the most beautiful in the avian world.

Each species of hummingbird has its own particular type of nest. Some are cone-shaped and others look like tiny cups. Many females use bits of bark for decoration, while others create fluffy, yet strong, nests that resemble cotton candy. Some hummingbirds, like the Anna's and Allen's, also make their nests in isolated areas far from those occupied by males or other females. Most, however, construct nests that blend in so perfectly with their surroundings that they are practically invisible to a person who may be standing only inches away and staring right at it.

Each species of hummingbirds constructs its own unique nest. Here we see those of the Anna's (RIGHT), *Allen's* (BELOW), *Costa's* (OPPOSITE, TOP) *and Black-chinned* (OPPOSITE, BOTTOM).

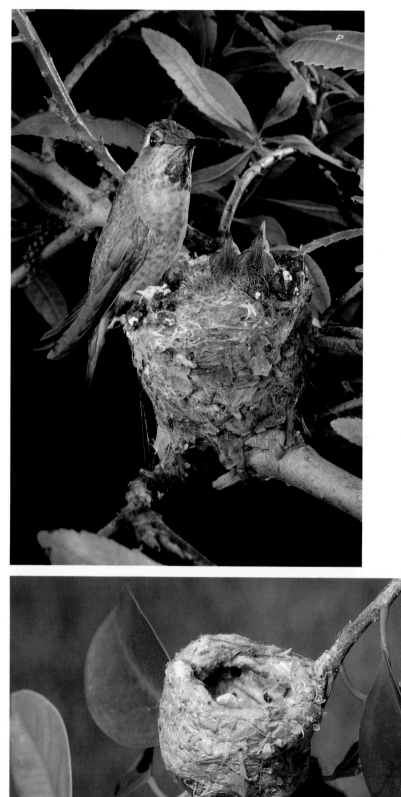

Locations vary. Some nests hang from ledges, while others are built on branches and still others can be found clinging to rocks. Some are even suspended by tendrils from nearby foliage.

The amount of light filtering through trees can make a difference in the location of a nest, too. Rufous Hummingbirds in British Columbia, for example, were found to build their nests at heights that fluctuated with light inten-

Female hummers often build their nests in unlikely places such as this Costa's did in a Cholla Cactus. Rancho Santa Ana Botanical Gardens, Claremont, California.

sity. When there was little light, they built their nests close to the ground, and when the light intensity was greater, they constructed them higher up.

At the core of a hummingbird's nest is a solid foundation around which various soft, strong materials such as spiderwebs and other fibers are wound. In the interior of the egg cups are extremely soft, thick linings made of cottony down, feathers, lichens or leaves. Moss, small roots, fern frond scales, bits of grass and long strands of hair from various plants are also used. At the San Diego Zoo, a female hummer, furnished with clippings of hairs from llamas and other exotic animals, disdained them all in favor of poodle fur.

Incredibly, early naturalists believed that the thick soft linings of tropical hummingbird nests were constructed not only to provide warm cushions for eggs but also, and more importantly, to protect them from the electrically charged atmosphere.

In 1841, R. Hill, Esq., sent a letter from Jamaica to the Zoological Society of London chiding the society for not having paid enough attention to the study of hummingbird nest construction with respect to protection of eggs from electricity. He likened the silky cocoons of various insects that were spun during hot climates to the nests of hummingbirds that were often observed breeding during the rainy season, a time when the skies were full of electrical charges. He believed that the active electricity caused by lightning from summer storms would quickly kill the developing embryos. Successful, undisturbed incubation of eggs during this time could only be accomplished, he felt, by wrapping them in organic materials that could not conduct electricity.

A female Ruby-throated will deposit her eggs in this nest, which has been carefully lined with thick cushiony layers of cobwebs, feathers, lichens and other organic materials. Sodus Bay, New York.

Hummingbirds fuse their various nesting materials together with cobwebs and other filaments and use these same fibers to attach the nest to its base. The exteriors of the nest are strong, firm and capable of keeping out moisture. Fortunately, nesting materials are also often flexible enough to stretch as the occupants grow, but at times a nest breaks open, dumping out nestlings it can no longer accommodate.

The exteriors of sturdy egg cups, which usually measure about 2 inches in diameter, are constructed and adorned with a variety of unusual materials that sometimes show the resourcefulness of the female hummingbird.

For example, an Anna's nest was discovered to be bound by rodent hairs, while that of an Allen's contained strands from the fur of squirrels, dogs and horses. The female Allen's also made use of fibers extracted from the inner roof of an old car parked nearby. In addition, Calliope and Anna's hummingbirds sometimes use insect cocoons as well as pine needles, fern scales and minute portions of insect and spider skeletons. Female hummers will also sometimes steal bits of organic matter from the nests, either in use or abandoned, of other larger birds and even other hummingbirds.

Hummingbirds use their breasts, bills and feet to build and repair their nests. Bills, which are used to carry bits of fluff and foliage, are particularly useful for poking, pulling and prodding materials into the nest. And hovering hummingbirds can sometimes be seen plucking filaments from organic downy puffs that are still making their way to the ground.

The bill is also used to weave material around the outside of the nest, while the cuplike form is made by pressing the breast against the nest's exterior as the female winds her way around it. A nest is also built in such a way so that its upper edge protrudes inward, forming a secure seal with the mother's body. The female also flattens the thick nest floor by running or jogging on it.

Most species of hummingbirds build new nests every year, although a very few, like the Calliope, make use of the old one by either refurbishing it with a fresh lining or building a completely new structure on top.

It can take a hummingbird from one day to two weeks to build a nest. In addition, many hummingbird mothers often continue to build up and decorate their nests after having laid their eggs.

THE CLUTCH

Since some species of hummingbirds are the smallest birds in the world, it should come as no surprise that they also lay the smallest eggs. Elliptical in shape, they usually measure less than $\frac{1}{2}$ inch and weigh less than $\frac{1}{2}$ gram. The egg of the ostrich, the largest bird, is also the largest, averaging $6\frac{1}{2}$ inches in length and 1,400 grams in weight. The eggs of a Giant Hummingbird weigh about $1\frac{1}{2}$ grams and measure 20 millimeters, making them the largest eggs among hummers.

If we keep in mind the small size of the female hummingbird, the eggs she lays are really quite large. In fact, the eggs may weigh 10–20 percent or more of her own weight, compared to only 2–4 percent in other larger birds. The two eggs of the Vervain Hummingbird, for example, make up an amazing 34 percent of the bird's total weight.

When freshly laid, hummingbird eggs have a pinkish cast to them and are translucent when held to a light. As the egg matures, it becomes more opaque. One early scientist declared that hummingbird eggs so resembled bon-bons that he thought it quite likely that someone might eat them thinking they were candy!

Hummingbirds nearly always lay two eggs. If there should ever be more than two in a clutch, however, it is probably because more than one female

The tiny egg of an Anna's Hummingbird is dwarfed by that of a chicken. Hummingbird eggs are the smallest in the avian world. Western Foundation of Vertebrate Zoology.

Incubating female Anna's will
spend 60 to 80 percent of the time
sitting on her eggs. Rancho Santa
Ana Botanical Gardens, Claremont,
California.

laid her eggs in the nest (perhaps because the nest of one was destroyed just as she was ready to lay them).

Female hummers tend to lay their eggs in the morning, and there is generally a two-day spread between laying of eggs. However, they also have been known (rarely) to lay their eggs anywhere from a day to three days apart.

When a bird sits on its eggs it is said to be incubating them. Eggs require a great deal of warmth (sometimes around 90° F) for proper development, and this high temperature is generated by the mother.

When the hummingbird female sits on her eggs, she fluffs out and separates her feathers so that the eggs are directly against her brood patch, a highly vascular area that transmits her body heat. The hummingbird sheds no feathers in forming this warm area, which is usually much less obvious than that of other birds.

Temperature sometimes determines the position of the incubating female in the nest. She will not leave her eggs when it is cold or rainy, and on these days she will fluff out her feathers and press herself especially close to give the eggs as much warmth as possible. When the weather is hot, she may hold her body and widespread tail off the eggs or stand inside the nest to shade them from the burning sun.

Eggs are turned at regular intervals in order to allow all sides to be warmed adequately. The mother will often use her bill to rotate them as she hovers alongside the nest, although when in it she may use her feet or her bill.

Periods of attentiveness range from three hours to less than a minute and hummingbird eggs are left unattended from 10 to 110 times per day. However, hummingbird mothers generally sit on their eggs from 60 to 80 percent of every day. Incubation periods are usually longer in the afternoon.

Eggs laid a couple of days apart will hatch at the same time only if the female does not begin incubating until she has laid the second one. Some species, however, automatically begin incubation when the first egg is laid.

Hummingbirds have an incubation period of approximately 15 to 22 days.

Surprisingly, the eggs of many species of songbirds actually have a shorter period of incubation than the hummingbird's tiny eggs, which take a relatively long time to hatch.

The developing embryo sustains itself on nutrients contained in the yolk and breathes by means of respiration during which oxygen and carbon dioxide pass through the porous shell.

NESTLINGS

When all the food within the egg has been consumed, all that remains is a chick that is ready to hatch. At this time, two unique physical features develop to aid the bird as it prepares to make its way into the outside world.

The first is the egg tooth, a calcareous projection found on the bill's tip that helps it peck through the shell. The other is a large hatching muscle that develops on the back of its head to provide greater force to the egg tooth. Once the bird has successfully hatched, both of these temporary features disappear.

When ready to emerge, the bird pokes at the shell with its bill, an action called pipping. When the chick has hatched, the only portion of the egg's interior that is left is the yolk sac, which provides nutrients for the next day or two. The yolk sac will later gradually be reabsorbed into the chick's body and become part of its intestinal wall.

Broken eggshells and any other egg remnants are cleaned up and disposed of by the mother, since they have an odor that could attract predators. Unhatched eggs remain in the nest.

The young of hummingbirds are altricial—that is, featherless, virtually helpless and in need of constant care. Baby hummingbirds, which are darkly pigmented at birth, are born with closed eyes and almost nonexistent bills. They are also psilopaedic, which means that they have just a few strands of down on their otherwise naked bodies and rely entirely on the mother for warmth. Unlike other birds, hummingbird nestlings do not acquire a downy coat. Instead, they develop pinfeathers after a few days and will not lose these feathers until after they fledge, whereupon they molt for the first time. Within 8 to 12 days after hatching, the young birds are able to maintain their own temperatures.

When a female sits on her nestlings, she is said to be brooding. Brooding periods among the different species of hummingbirds range from 12 to 18 days, during which babies are fed from 1.2 to 3 times every hour. Weather is a factor in determining the length of brooding periods; they will be longer if external temperatures are very low.

Nestlings begin begging instinctively even before their eyes open. The sound of the mother's whirring wings or the sensation of movement within the nest will cause the babies to gape. In addition, the linings of their mouths are brightly colored, creating a stimulus for the female to feed them.

As a rule, chicks are fed the same things that parents eat. In the case of little hummingbirds, food consists of regurgitated nectar and insects. This food is passed, or pumped, from the crop of the mother to those of her babies. Sometimes after a particularly ambitious feeding bout, the crops of the young birds will distend into large protruding lumps on either side of their necks.

The interiors of hummingbird nests are clean. After hatching, the mother either tosses feces overboard, carries them away or eats them. Later, older nestlings will expel feces over the nest's edge like baby hawks. Even though a hummingbird chick is small, it will instinctively make its way to the rim of the nest in order to eject its excrement, even if it means standing on its head while holding steadfast to the nest wall.

Experiments with nesting Anna's and Calliope hummingbirds have shown that neither they nor their nestlings go into torpor on chilly nights. In fact, a female hummingbird is capable of sustaining a temperature within the nest that is 40° to 54° F higher than the cold temperatures outside. Nestlings can maintain their own high temperatures once they have reached the age of 8 to 12 days and at times are left to pass cold nights unattended.

It has been suggested that a female that is incubating does not have to become torpid because she feeds herself very well before sundown. Also, she may have a lower metabolic rate. It is also possible that she is able to conserve more energy, since she is relatively inactive throughout most of the day and most of the body heat that would be lost from the front surface of her body is retained when she sits on the nest. In addition, it has been found that Calliope Hummingbirds and other species that nest in climates where the temperature approaches freezing are able to construct nests capable of keeping heat loss to a minimum.

A heat sensor placed between two eggs in an Anna's Hummingbird's nest to measure the temperature of their surfaces measured approximately 50° F higher than external temperatures during evening hours. Later, once the 13-day-old nestlings could thermoregulate themselves, the nest registered over 86° F above outside temperatures.

The nest of another incubating Anna's was fitted with heat sensors and determined to have an average temperature of 89.4° F during daylight hours with an average 81.5° F in the evening. When she was not on the nest, temperatures ranged from 109.4° F to 56.7° F.

Costa's mother feeds her chicks regurgitated nectar and insects. Santa Monica Mountains, California.

This female Costa's pumps food directly into the crops of her young. Rancho Santa Ana Botanical Gardens, Claremont, California.

Hummingbird nestlings, such as these two Costa's, can maintain their own temperatures once they are 8 to 12 days old and are sometimes left to pass cold nights unattended.

Twenty-one days seems to be the norm for hummingbird nestlings to remain in the nest, although some species, like the Ruby-throated, may stay as long as 31 days. Forty to 65 days was found to be the range during which females continued to feed their chicks after hatching, but this included caring for them after they had fledged.

Infertile eggs or those that die during development remain in the nest. In a study of Broad-tailed Hummingbirds, some were found to continue incubating infertile eggs up to four days past the time they should have hatched, and it is believed that the females were aware of the fact that they were overdue. In addition, there is a report of an Anna's Hummingbird that incubated infertile eggs for 95 days. In another instance, a Broad-tailed female continued to brood her dead chick for a day after it had died.

Hummingbird chicks grow more rapidly when raised in areas where there is an abundant food supply than in regions where flowers are not as plentiful.

Surprisingly, females in captivity have been known to care for chicks they did not bear. And White-eared Hummingbirds in the wild have been seen caring for both their own and other nestlings.

Hummingbird young preen their new feathers and appear alert at about 16 days. In addition to grooming themselves with their bills and feet, they also exercise their wings and tongues and will gingerly touch nearby plants

After about 16 days, little hummingbirds start stretching their wings. Note the juvenal plumage growing on this Black-chinned youngster. Van Nuys, California.

Costa's chick flapping its wings. Santa Monica Mountains, California.

Costa's nestlings exploring each
other and nearby cactus. Rancho
Santa Ana Botanical Gardens,
Claremont, California.

Fledgling Costa's hummers preening. Rancho Santa Ana Botanical Gardens, Claremont, California.

and twigs. When trying their wings for the first time, fledgling hummingbirds appear to stand on tiptoe but in reality are anchoring themselves to the nest's edge.

It is not necessary for female hummers to push their children from the nest. When ready to leave, the fledglings often choose the morning hours for their first flights, which are sometimes over 50 feet. They are really quite proficient at flying almost immediately, although they may have a lot of trouble landing. We once followed one and noted that although it could fly quite well, it had difficulty achieving any height and was unable to climb more than 5 feet off the ground.

Hummingbirds who have left the nest will sometimes continue to be fed and preened by their mothers. These curious youngsters will automatically try many types of flowers before they discover those particular ones that produce plenty of nectar. Once they are sufficiently on their own, the mother will force them out of her territory unless she happens to leave first.

Although female hummingbirds generally raise one brood at a time, there are exceptions. Black-chinned, Ruby-throated and White-eared hummingbirds, for example, have been known to care for two nests simultaneously.

Also, two nests, situated almost 4 feet apart, were reported being cared for by a Ruby-throated Hummingbird. One contained eggs, which she incubated, and the other held a brood, which she fed and defended against intruders.

In another instance, a Black-chinned female began building a second nest approximately 40 feet from her first nest, which held already-hatched chicks. After her first brood had departed, she incubated the second family. Another Black-chinned female was discovered caring for three nests during one breeding season, two of them simultaneously.

Those species of hummingbirds that rear two broods generally do not finish with one nest before building the second. Rather, the second is usually constructed while care of the first brood continues.

Blue-throated, Allen's and Black-chinned hummingbirds all may nest more than once in a season, and the Anna's may often raise three broods in

ANNA'S NESTING SEQUENCE—
RANCHO SANTA ANA
BOTANICAL GARDENS
Female Anna's stands guard over
her nest of five-day-old chicks. Note
the long downy filaments on their
backs. Rancho Santa Ana Botanical
Gardens, Claremont, California.

that time. In fact, it is entirely possible (although up to now undocumented) that all species have multiple broodings.

Hummingbird mothers are fearless when it comes to defending their nests and have been known to attack such large predators as hawks and crows. Chipmunks, scrub jays, snakes and yellow jackets also plunder these nests, since they are fond of both hummingbird eggs and nestlings.

Surprisingly, while hummingbirds are quite defensive and aggressively guard their young against animals, they can be quite docile when it comes to man. For example, when Robert was photographing an Anna's nest that was situated on a branch 6 feet high, the female, after a lengthy inspection of the ladder, sandbags, tripod, camera and lights, blithely went about her business while the rest of us struggled to make sure he photographed successfully without tumbling down.

She feeds her blind, hungry babies.
Note their yellow bills.

These 12-day-old nestlings, which gaped instinctively almost immediately after hatching, continue to do so when they sense their mother's presence.

The insides of the babies' mouths are brightly colored, apparently stimulating the mother to feed them.

The whirring of the mother's wings, too, will cause these 19-day-old chicks to beg.

At 26 days, the young birds are reaching a time when they will no longer be fed by their mother.

Snug and warm, these 26-day-old
nestlings await the return of their
mother. They were on their own
only a few days later.

*A CAPTIVE ANNA'S GIVES
BIRTH IN THE JEWEL ROOM
OF THE SAN DIEGO ZOO*
*The first hummingbird in six years
to breed in captivity at the San
Diego Zoo, this female Anna's
patiently waits for her egg to hatch.*

She feeds her five-day-old chick, who nestles in a warm nest of poodle fur. She disdained llama fur and other exotic furs she was given.

At five days, this chick instinctively expels its feces over the nest's edge.

The female calmly feeds her nestling, whose eyes have still not opened after 13 days.

The female continues to build up her nest as her chick grows bigger.

After 20 days the bird has grown so large the female has difficulty finding a place to sit.

With her little one safe and warm beneath her, she continues building up and repairing her nest.

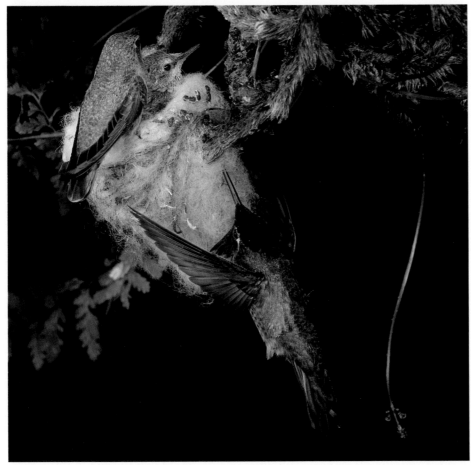

The male Anna's, which generally leaves the female alone after mating, suddenly appears after 20 days. It continually tries to attack and poke the young nestling until the female is finally successful in driving him away.

After fledging, the young bird continues to be fed and cared for by its mother.

On its own at last, the fledgling perches quietly.

Startled while feeding from the Beard Tongue (PENSTEMON BARBATUS), a Broad-tailed hummer scatters nectar droplets throughout the air.

Food and Metabolism | 7

They feed by thrusting their Bill and Tongue into the blossoms of Trees, and so
suck the sweet Juice of Honey from them; and when he sucks he sits not, but
bears up his Body with a hovering Motion of his Wings. . . .

Nehemiah Grew, M.D.
Philosophical Transactions
1693

Watching a hummingbird feed delicately from a blossom, one might never guess the tremendous amount of energy that is required to keep the tiny aerial dynamo going. And since it is usually difficult to observe a hummingbird going about its daily activities, many aspects of its feeding and sleeping behavior are relatively unknown to most people.

These particular activities, however, have been carefully studied and have proved to be quite intriguing.

The complex process by which food consumed is turned into energy is known as metabolism. The metabolic rate is the rate at which food consumed is metabolized, or used, by an animal. With respect to birds, it varies with each species and changes in accordance with their movements. For example, it is lower when the bird is resting and higher when it is active.

The standard, or basal, metabolic rate allows one to compare rates of metabolism among birds of distinct species. This figure is calculated to reflect the amount of heat generated by a resting bird during a 24-hour period and is measured in calories per kilogram.

Since the systems of smaller birds operate at faster rates than those of larger ones, their metabolic rates are higher. For example, both heart and respiratory rates of hummingbirds are very rapid and their weight-specific metabolic rates are also very high. In fact, only those of insects are greater.

Compared to other birds, the rates of hummingbirds are fantastic. For example, a 4-gram hummingbird has a basic metabolic rate of 1,400 calories per kilogram. A 121-gram Mourning Dove has a rate of 127 calories per kilogram, and a 10-gram wren has a rate of 589 calories per kilogram. The weight-specific metabolism of a hummingbird in repose is 25 times that of a domestic fowl and 12 times that of a pigeon.

Among all birds that eat nectar, the standard metabolic rates of hummingbirds are about 3 to $3\frac{1}{2}$ times the norm.

If man had as high a weight-specific metabolic rate as a hummingbird, his daily intake of food would have to be approximately twice his body weight. Also, his temperature would be over 750° F and he would use up 155,000 calories per day.

Because their weight-specific metabolic rates are extremely high, hummingbirds require great quantities of food, relatively speaking. Indeed, it has been suggested that it would be impossible for a warm-blooded animal that was smaller than a hummingbird to exist, since it would be impossible for it to consume enough food to supply its tremendous energy requirements.

A hummingbird requires an adequate diet of protein, carbohydrates, fats, vitamins and minerals, and its primary source of food is nectar, which is usually found at the base of the corollas of certain flowers. The long, narrow bills and extrusile tongues of the hummingbirds are well adapted to feeding efficiently from these nectar-rich blossoms.

The long narrow bill and extrusile tongue of the hummingbird enable it to probe deep into corollas of tubular flowers. Here the tongue of a male Anna's feeding from the Chuparosa (BELOPERONE CALIFORNICA) misses its mark.

Hummingbirds are not the only birds that feed on nectar. Hawaiian Honeycreepers, Sunbirds and Honey Eaters also feed from flowers, but they do so from a perched position, since they are unable to hover.

Nectar, which is composed of various sugars that are digested easily and quickly converted into energy, supplies a hummingbird's carbohydrate requirements as well as, possibly, necessary amino acids.

The amount of nectar in a flower and its sugar concentration determine the amount of energy the hummingbird will derive from it. Ingestion is accomplished by a licking motion of the tongue at a rate of about 13 per second, and the larger the tongue, the more liquid is consumed with each lick.

Insects are also part of a hummingbird's diet. Sometimes, while appearing to pirouette through the air, hummingbirds will snatch insects with their long bills. Others pick them from both inside and outside flowers and from underneath leaves. They are also often hunted along walls, trees or flower bushes, and filmy webs are sometimes plundered for minute spiders or their prey. Some hummingbirds have even been seen stealing the quarry of giant tropical spiders.

Insects provide protein, minerals, vitamins and fats and are digested more slowly than nectar. Nevertheless, it takes only ten minutes for the remains of some insects to pass completely through the hummingbird's body.

When it rains, hummingbirds appear to increase their preference for insects. They will also naturally eat more of them when flowers are no longer abundant. In Texas, for example, Blue-throated Hummingbirds were observed consuming a diet that was made up exclusively of insects when their nectar reserves had been exhausted.

In addition, Colombian and Brazilian species feed on certain secretions known as honeydew. A sweet, viscous liquid, honeydew is transmitted through narrow waxen tubes by coccid insects that live underneath the bark of certain trees. It has been estimated that one hummingbird can successfully feed daily during winter months from a tree that contains 5,000 of these insects.

There are four species of North American hummingbirds that in addition to eating nectar and insects eat the sugary sap found in holes made by the Yellow-bellied Sapsucker. There are also rare accounts of hummingbirds feeding from fruits and berries.

On eleven different occasions, hummingbirds were seen eating sand. Since eight of these instances involved female hummers, it was felt that they might be supplementing their diets with calcium for eggs or perhaps replacing calcium that had been lost in laying them.

Naturally, hummingbirds also require water. Most is supplied through nectar, although sometimes the birds will drink from wet leaves after bathing. One experiment with captive hummingbirds indicated that they need four to five times as much water as solid food, as evidenced by their frequent trips to a fountain to supplement their water ration.

These tiny birds also consume great quantities of food, relatively, every day to provide enough fuel for their metabolism. About 50 percent of its weight in sugar is probably eaten daily by a hummingbird (not 200 percent, as was once believed).

When mixing sugar water for commercial feeders, the best ratio is 1 part sugar to 5 parts water, since this closely approximates the concentrations found in the nectar of the wildflowers they prefer. Wild hummers will feed happily from this sweet solution and supplement their protein requirement by finding an adequate supply of insects.

Feeders of hummingbirds kept in captivity, on the other hand, are often filled with a specially formulated dietary supplement known as Hydramin, which compensates for the lack of insects that often occurs.

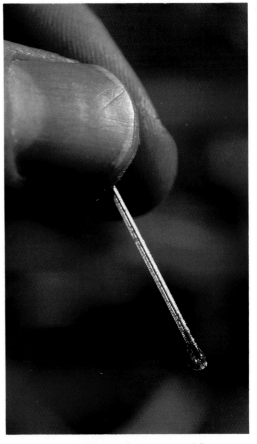

Pipette of nectar tapped from blossom of the Scarlet Penstemon (PENSTEMON LABROSUS). *Nectar supplies a hummingbird with carbohydrates and, possibly, amino acids.*

An acquaintance of ours, a Venezuelan ornithologist, indicated that he kept hummingbirds thriving in captivity without insects or special additives. His secret? A single drop of cow's blood in each feeder.

How many calories per day are used by a hummingbird? Well, daily energy expenditures of some hummingbird species have been found to range from 6,660 to 12,400. The bigger the hummingbird, the more total calories it

The hummingbird, which has a very high weight-specific metabolic rate, gets most of its energy from nectar. Male Anna's feeding from Ocotillo (FOUQUIERIA SPLENDENS).

Hummingbirds hover while feeding from nectar-rich blossoms that generally lack appendages for sitting. Whenever possible, however, they will save energy by eating while perched. Male Anna's, Ocotillo (FOUQUIERIA SPLENDENS).

uses. A hovering 10-gram hummer, for example, uses approximately 35 calories per minute. A 3-gram hummingbird was found to expend 10.8 calories per minute. A hovering bumblebee burned 0.5 calorie in the same time.

In addition, extra energy must be stored if a hummingbird does not enter torpor. A total of 10,300 calories were expended by an Anna's Hummingbird during a day when he slept normally compared to 7,600 calories when he went torpid.

Calorie Expenditure of Wild Male Anna's Hummingbird—12 Hours, 52 Minutes
(Average Day)

Activity	Calories
Perching	3,810
Capturing insects	90
Foraging for nectar	2,460
Territorial aggression	300

A hummingbird would have to visit 1,022 fuchsia blossoms to get enough nectar to enable it to perform all the above activities, which require a total energy expenditure of 6,660 calories.

A great many flowers have developed plentiful stores of nectar with which to attract hummingbirds. In return, they rely on these little birds for pollination.

Hummingbirds feed from these flowers from a hovering position, since most of these nectar-rich blossoms are not structured in such a way as to allow for a place to perch. Whenever possible, however, a hummingbird will sit in order to conserve energy.

Any nectar-producing flower can provide nourishment to hummingbirds, but they prefer certain types. Blossoms on these favored flowers are arranged far enough apart so that the bird can successfully probe interiors without hitting parts of other flowers as it hovers.

Hummingbirds will also harvest nectar from flowers of all colors, although those they are usually seen feeding from are often red (or in the red to violet portion of the spectrum), tubular and odorless. Red flowers can, by virtue of their color, exclude such competitors as bees that generally prefer flowers from the violet range of the spectrum. Flowers pollinated by hummingbirds in the western portion of the United States are usually red.

As a rule, hummingbirds will stay at a flower as long as it takes to tap its sweet syrup, a process that sometimes takes only a moment but sometimes much longer, depending upon the amount of nectar held in the blossom.

It is interesting to note that larger blooms seem to be visited by the larger hummers and the smaller plants by the smaller species.

Flower nectars vary according to the amount produced by the flower and the sugar concentration. A plant that produces a nectar that is too rich in sugar will satisfy its pollinator too quickly and consequently will not be pollinated as effectively.

In 1974, it was stated that hummingbirds and butterflies most often were attracted to flowers with nectars that had higher concentrations of sugar than other flowers. Although this has been disputed, it has been determined that flowers from which hummingbirds feed usually have an average 20 to 25 percent concentration of sugar.

Compared to other birds, hummingbirds have the highest degree of food assimilation. In fact, almost 100 percent of the sugar consumed by a hummingbird is absorbed into its body.

Sugar solutions for commercial feeders of 1 part sugar to 5 parts water best approximate the sugar concentrations of wildflower nectars preferred by hummingbirds. Rufous feeding from Monkey-flower (MIMULUS CARDINALIS).

In contrast, assimilation among other birds ranges between 30 and 99 percent. For example, owls, which eat meat, utilized 68 to 88 percent of their food, and Song Sparrows and cardinals, which eat seeds, utilized 49 to 89 percent.

Some of the food eaten by hummers is immediately used, but a portion may sometimes be stored in the crop for future needs such as maintaining temperature during torpor.

Hummingbirds do not have an instinctive knowledge of which flowers to visit. In fact, their selection of flowers is a learned process.

Apparently by using trial and error, they are soon able to recognize the structure, color and taste of certain favorite blossoms. In fact, the bird can tell after only one visit to a bird feeder or blossom whether or not it is worth returning to.

Several experiments have been conducted to determine how humming-birds choose their favorite flowers. Results show that a nectar's sugar concentration is more important than the color of the container holding it. Nor will they continue to visit feeders with solutions made up of less than 1 part sugar to 8 parts water. Sugar concentration was also found to be more important than either the location of the food or the amount of sugar released by the feeder. And they also preferred sugar water from feeders that had short rather than long corollas, since more nectar per visit was thus released to them.

In order of preference, hummingbirds like sucrose, glucose and fructose. Black-chinned Hummingbirds chose white sugar over processed honey and liked brown sugar least of all. Hummers will also shun feeders that contain pure glucose or fructose.

The location of a food source is clearly an important factor as well. Experiments have shown that hummingbirds will continue to choose feeders that are in certain areas even though the color of the syrup has been changed. Surprisingly, it was also discovered that when the food was removed, the birds continued to defend the foodless territory for three days both frequently and aggressively.

In order of preference, an Anna's Hummingbird was found to prefer sugar water in red, yellow, green, clear and blue feeders. After becoming accustomed to abundant supplies of food from containers of certain colors, hummingbirds will subsequently visit flasks and flowers of the same color.

Hummingbirds do not use their sense of smell in locating food, nor does it aid them in bypassing flowers that are poisonous. For example, oleander flowers were disdained only after the birds tried them first and found them unpleasant to the taste.

Hummers search for food, or forage, in a variety of ways. Some defend specific territories and others do not. During the late 1970s an experiment isolated the foraging activities of 21 Mexican hummingbirds. Some were found to be *trapliners*. These were roving hummingbirds who did not establish territories and fed from many different kinds of flowers. There were also *territorial* hummingbirds who migrated to certain areas. Since they required more sugar, they were found to feed from flowers that produced more nectar. They also consumed insects. *Residents* inhabited an area all year long and selected tubular flowers as their mainstay. They formed territories that they defended.

There are other foraging characteristics common among tropical species as well. These include two types of trapliners. The first, the *high-reward trapliners,* have bills that have been adapted to feed from particular flowers. They continuously feed from certain blossoms until there is no more nectar, and they are nonterritorial. *Low-reward trapliners,* on the other hand, have bills that are neither as long nor as curved, and they feed from a variety of flowers.

In addition, there are *territorialists*. These territorial hummingbirds do not limit themselves to certain flowers but rather visit all they can within a specific region. *Territory parasites* can be large or small and feed freely from those areas controlled by other hummingbird species.

In addition, some hummingbirds engage in *peripheral foraging.* It has been found that nectar levels of flowers located in the outer half of the territories of Rufous Hummingbirds are highest in early morning. Invading hummingbirds feeding from these blossoms during this time of day could severely deplete the owner's necessary food supply. The Rufous Hummingbird begins feeding in this outer region first, thus reducing the nectar supply to lower levels than even those found in flowers deep within its territory. The bird forages indiscriminately among all remaining flowers for the rest of the day.

It has been found that hummingbirds that create and defend territories have superior flight abilities. Traplining hummers, however, hover more efficiently, since they require less energy to do so. The proportion of wingspread during hovering to the bird's weight is called wing disc loading, and that of a traplining hummingbird is lower. In addition, its wings are longer.

Only 16 percent of the foraging time of seven species of nonhermit hummingbirds is spent in capturing insects; the remaining 84 percent is spent in seeking and eating nectar. Among other kinds of hummingbirds, 14 percent of foraging time was spent capturing insects and 86 percent finding and eating nectar.

The amount of food ingested during the first meal of the day and the amount of energy burned between subsequent meals determines how frequently the hummingbird feeds. On an average, though, they feed five to eight times per hour. Those in captivity were found to feed every 10 minutes. Some also feed intensively just before dark. Feeding times are also partly related to the weather, and it is unlikely they feed during severe storms.

In an experiment with Anna's and Rufous hummingbirds, it was discovered that both gained weight steadily as the day progressed. In the afternoon, both flew only 15 to 47 percent as often as they did during the morning, and most of this flying activity was to feed. Because they flew less, they naturally gained weight. The Anna's gained 16.4 percent in weight and the Rufous 10.8 percent.

Needless to say, Ruby-throated Hummingbirds have long amazed hummingbird observers with their 500-mile nonstop flight across the Gulf of Mexico. These birds burn tremendous amounts of energy when flying, but their size limits the amount of fat they can store. This little bird adds up to 40 to 50 percent of extra fat to its body weight for use in this marathon journey. It has been calculated that a 26-hour nonstop flight can be made by a male at 25 mph if the bird burns only 2 grams of fat.

The daily oxygen consumption of hummingbirds is also enormous. For example, in a study of five different species, they were found to consume oxygen at hourly rates ranging from 42 to 147 cubic centimeters per gram of body weight. When hovering steadily for 35 minutes, a Costa's consumed 42.4 cubic centimeters per gram per hour. Also, seven times more oxygen is used by a hovering hummingbird than a perching one.

The range in temperature between a hummingbird that is active and one in repose is really very small, and when it is sleeping normally the temperature lowers only approximately 4° to 8° F.

Since hummingbirds do not feed after dark and their plumage does not provide adequate warmth, it would be disastrous for them to pass particularly cold nights without some form of energy conservation. In order for them to achieve this, some hummers, both wild and in captivity, lower their temperatures and metabolic rates and become torpid.

In 1651 it was written in the *Penny Cyclopaedia* that hummingbirds "were supposed to live no longer than the flowers which afforded them food; and, when those flowers faded, they were believed to fix themselves by the bill to some pine or other tree, and there remain during the dreary months till the descending rains brought back the spring, when they revived again to undergo the same alteration of life and death."

While today one might smile at such an erroneous deduction, it is easy to see how a hummingbird in torpor could be mistaken for dead.

Chilean hummers were once dubbed "resurrected" birds because they were speedily aroused from torpid states by being warmed within the bosoms of women. Indeed, seventeenth-century New World Indians were given the familiar illustration of hummingbirds seemingly being brought back from the dead to convey the idea of the Resurrection.

Some species of bats, rodents and birds also go torpid, as well as reptiles, which do so when hibernating. Fish and amphibians, too, can enter this state, thought to be a function of the central nervous system, when food is scarce.

If a hummingbird remains outdoors during a night when the temperature dips to below freezing, it, too, runs the risk of freezing. For this reason,

The diminutive Ruby-throated
Hummingbird stores up an
astonishing 40–50 percent extra fat
of its body weight to supply it with
the energy necessary to travel 500
miles nonstop across the Gulf of
Mexico.

Torpid hummingbirds were once known as "resurrected" birds because they appeared to rise from the dead. Anna's Hummingbird.

some species, such as the Andean Hillstar, find shelter in such places as mine shafts and caves.

It was once believed that hummingbirds automatically went into torpor every night, but this theory has been disproved. In fact, it is not unusual to see two hummers of the same species pass the night with one going torpid and the other only sleeping.

A hummingbird's energy reserves as well as its health determine whether or not it will go into torpor. Outside temperatures are also a factor, since torpidity among hummingbirds does not occur at temperatures of 95° F or higher. If the bird is in a molting state, there is also a greater likelihood that it will become torpid.

Some species prepare for the evening by simply storing up extra fuel and thus do not have to go into torpor. For example, in an experiment with Anna's and Rufous hummingbirds, the Anna's automatically ate more and stored more fat and were thus able to avoid going into torpor. The Rufous, however, did not eat more, lowered their body temperatures during the day and became torpid in the evening.

Blue-throated hummer fluffs out his feathers in preparation for sleep.

A hummingbird may also go torpid for only part of a night, if necessary.

It is thought that incubating females will enter torpor if their energy supply has been severely depleted.

In actuality, no hummingbird will become torpid unless it is absolutely necessary for survival during the night, for it is the bird's last resort against expiring from lack of food reserves. It may exhibit a reluctance to do so because of the inherent danger involved in going into such a state, since it then becomes defenseless against its nocturnal enemies. There is also always the possibility that it may not awaken.

Sometimes, just before going into torpor, the bird will fluff out its feathers in order to let excess heat escape and allow it to lower its body tempera-

The metabolic rate of a torpid hummingbird ranges from $1/50$ to $1/60$ that of one that is awake, and it is believed that some species are capable of controlling their temperatures to keep them from dipping too low. Broad-billed, Lucifer, Broad-tailed and Ruby-throated hummingbirds.

ture more quickly. The larger the hummingbird, the longer it takes to become torpid.

The metabolic rate of a torpid hummingbird is usually no less than $\frac{1}{5}$ of one sleeping normally and ranges from $\frac{1}{50}$ to $\frac{1}{60}$ that of an awake but resting hummer.

Body temperatures of tropical hummingbirds were found to range from a normal 102° to 106° F when particularly active and around 93° to 95° F when torpid or sleeping.

It is believed that many species of hummingbirds can control their body temperatures during torpidity. For example, when outside temperatures fell below 64° F a torpid Purple-throated Carib was able to maintain its temperature at 64° to 68° F through its ability to regulate its oxygen consumption.

It has been suggested that this control of temperature and oxygen consumption is not only for purposes of energy conservation but may also prevent the levels from dipping to such low points that the bird becomes incapable of being aroused at all. Also, by keeping its temperature regulated at a certain level, the hummingbird will awaken more easily from torpor, since the higher its temperature, the easier it is to come out of it.

A hummingbird in torpor resembles a stiff corpse. It does not function normally and can sometimes cry softly but definitely cannot fly. It also practically freezes its grip on whatever twig it may be perched on.

The lower the energy reserve, the more readily it will enter the torpid state and the more lengthy will be the period of torpor, which normally can range from 8 to 14 hours.

During torpidity, breathing becomes less regular and may, in fact, cease completely if outside temperatures become low enough.

Both water and oxygen are conserved by a hummingbird when it is torpid. Indeed, $\frac{1}{3}$ to $\frac{1}{10}$ the average evaporative water loss is lost during torpor.

With respect to oxygen consumption, 6.4 milliliters of oxygen per gram per hour are conserved by the Purple-throated Carib when it is torpid. At the same temperature, it uses twice as much when not torpid.

Heart rate also changes during torpidity according to temperatures reached in that state. Heart rates of torpid hummingbirds have been measured at 48 to 180 beats per minute.

Sound, touch or light can awaken a torpid hummingbird as well as some possible internal body signal. Sometimes a hummingbird will come out of torpor before the sun rises, while others must wait until the sun has warmed them sufficiently.

It may take a hummer over an hour to be aroused. Its temperature rises at a rate of about 1 to 1.5 degrees every minute. As it is being aroused, also, there is a quickening of its heart and breathing rates. The larger the hummingbird, the slower it awakens.

Flight becomes possible only after body temperature has reached levels of 86° F or higher.

Weight loss also occurs when birds become torpid, as evidenced by experiments involving Black-chinned and Magnificent hummingbirds, which were found to weigh less the following morning.

In the nurtured environments of zoos, hummingbirds have lived up to $10\frac{1}{2}$ years. Banded Brazilian hummers have survived at least 9 years and there have even been reports of Blue-throated Hummingbirds living up to 12 years.

Do hummingbirds show their age? Well, several years ago, the head keeper of the Jewel Room at the New York Zoological Park attested to the fact that its 8-year-old Garnet-throated Hummingbird had pronounced bags and wrinkles!

It may take a torpid hummingbird (TOP) over an hour to be aroused, and its temperature rises at a rate of 1 to 1¹/₂ degrees every minute. Once awake, it stretches (BOTTOM) and feeds almost immediately. Male Anna's.

Intruder thirstily pilfers nectar from territory of another hummingbird, unaware of the angry owner, who is homing in for an attack. Two female Rufous, Scarlet Penstemon (PENSTEMON LABROSUS).

Behavior

*They are very fond of chasing one another, sometimes for sport, often for spite.
. . . At such times I am always reminded of a lot of schoolboys playing tag.*

F. Stephens
*Bulletin of the Ridgway
Ornithological Club of Chicago*
April 1887

Although hummingbirds are somewhat antisocial, they are definitely inquisitive and quarrelsome, and watching them go about their daily activities can be great fun. They are also noisy.

A hummingbird in the wild is often heard before it is seen. Its voice, which is not particularly loud, can best be described as a chatter, the range of which extends from a deep guttural sound to the highest of chirps and can sometimes even reach into frequencies that humans cannot hear. In addition, many species and genera do not sing under any circumstances.

Hummingbird songs, which enable them to communicate with others, are usually sung by males which in establishing and protecting territories often sing from high perches, allowing their musical warnings to be heard over long distances and at the same time giving them a better view of the activities taking place on their turf. Unfortunately, the songs of the hummingbird are not very pretty. In fact, that of the Anna's brings to mind a nail being scratched along the inside of a rusty tin can. Those of the other North American species are not much better, although the Costa's ends its song with a distinctive haunting whistle.

Happily, there are at least three exceptions. The most beautiful songs are said to be those of the Wedge-tailed Sabrewing, whose melodious tunes have prompted some to dub it the "nightingale" or "singing" hummingbird. And the soft, musical songs of the Vervain and the Wine-throated hummingbirds are also lovely.

A hummingbird sometimes sings quietly to itself or hums. This unusual sound, created without opening its bill, is easily detected, for when the bird produces it, it greatly enlarges its throat, points its bill upward and rounds out its back. Scaly-breasted male nestlings, as well as those of the Purple-throated Mountain-gem, often create these soft tones when feeding, as do some individuals engaged in courtship assemblies.

Most hummingbirds, such as those in courtship assemblies whose repertoire consists of a few strident repetitive notes, learn their songs. Once in a while, we will hear of one species singing the song of another species. For example, a Blue-chested Hummingbird was heard singing the distinctive and very different song of the Rufous-tailed Hummingbird.

In addition, the songs of the male Anna's Hummingbird of Guadalupe Island, off the coast of Baja California, were found to differ from those of the same species on the mainland. The mainland hummers did not respond to tape recordings of the island birds. It was suggested that the songs differed because the Anna's population on the island consists mostly of young males that had no adults from which to learn their songs.

Hummingbirds compete fiercely with other birds and even insects for nectar, and some species have developed a distinctive territorial foraging behavior.

A hummingbird often perches on a high branch near a flowering bush or feeder, thereby establishing it as its own. This elevated position, as mentioned earlier, affords it an excellent vantage point from which to assess the area. A hummingbird must determine that it will satisfy its daily energy requirements before it will take the area over as its own.

In establishing ownership, a hummingbird is assured of an abundant supply of food and possibly protection, for it rapidly becomes very familiar with the predators that also may live there.

The Anna's Hummingbird relies upon vocal warnings and air assaults to protect its turf. It announces its presence to other hummingbirds by singing a squeaky song, which also conveys the message that it is the owner. In addition, it often plumps up its feathers to appear bigger and more threatening. This gorget display, as it is called, is accompanied by an intense tossing of its resplendent head, the raising of the feathers that border the gorget and a soft, shrill note.

Rival hummingbirds, hearing the song, generally take heed and do not attempt to feed from the forbidden area. However, an intruder who ignores the warning runs a very real risk of being chased out or actually attacked. Hummingbirds that have just fed are slower to defend their territory than hungry ones.

A loud, chattering noise is uttered by an angry bird whose territory is even momentarily invaded. Generally, the owner has the advantage, particularly if the altercation takes place deep within its territory. The intruder, hearing the angry calls, knows that it will soon be descended upon and usually escapes. Rarely is a perching hummingbird attacked, the unfortunate victim nearly always being the airborne trespasser.

A hummingbird will vigorously chase and attack any creature, regardless of size, that dares to feed from its food source. Indeed, territories are often little more than battlegrounds.

Hummingbirds usually chase trespassers out of the territory, but sometimes direct physical combat ensues. These fights are rarely serious and birds are seldom harmed. Sometimes, however, a hummingbird can be seen with several back feathers missing, the result of a tussle.

The bill has often been considered too delicate an organ to risk being used as a weapon. However, on many occasions we have seen hummingbirds go straight for the eyes of enemy hummers with their bills in an attempt, perhaps, to pierce or gouge them out. The claws are used to grasp and

Brilliant coloration of the iridescent gorget and a threatening flying stance, such as that of this Ruby-throated Hummingbird, are used by hummingbirds in displays of aggression against other birds of their own and other species.

153

Although the claws are generally the hummingbird's weapons, the bill is also sometimes utilized. This airborne Ruby-throated is going straight for the eye of his perched enemy.

pummel each other with. Also, if the feuding pair is close enough, it is possible to hear the loud smack that results when they collide.

Sometimes fighting can be so intense that the pair, locked in a hostile grip, will fall to the ground and lie as though stunned, then rise within moments to resume their fierce battle.

It takes a hummingbird longer to defend a territory it has only recently acquired (within one or two days) than after the territory has been firmly established. Also, immature hummers fight longer than adults, and longer chases are engaged in by those hummingbirds of duller plumage than their brighter counterparts. These latter birds, however, appear to ward off intruders more effectively, trespassers appearing hesitant to enter the territories over which they preside.

Hummingbirds are antisocial and can be particularly belligerent during the breeding season, when they establish territories. In this sequence (pp. 155–57), a flying Ruby-throated Hummingbird vigorously attacks a perched male of the same species until finally successful in forcing him off the twig.

In this set of photos (pp. 158–60), two brilliantly colored Lucifers also battle for the one perch. It is easy to see the role that iridescent coloration plays in aggression. In the fifth photograph note that the aggressor actually grabs the bill of the surprised defender!

160

When its territory has an abundant food supply, an Anna's Hummingbird will not hesitate to descend aggressively upon any interloper. However, when food is scarce, its song and head movements become the primary form of aggression and the bird will limit its chases and aerial assaults, presumably to save energy.

Again, when nectar is scarce, a hummingbird will not pursue intruders past the limits of its territories as it would otherwise. Instead, it conserves energy by slackening its pace and engaging in shorter aerial pursuits.

A hummingbird will continue defending an area where the food supply is obviously diminishing through time and will even protect its territory for a while when it no longer yields any food. In order to compensate for this lack of nectar it will disappear for long periods, during which it is probably feeding elsewhere.

A hummingbird with dull plumage is better equipped to pilfer nectar under the watchful eye of another hummer than is one with brighter feathers. Size has also been found to be a factor in successful territorial defense, since the best-held territories are those of the larger species.

When defending their flowers, hummingbirds do not discriminate among their enemies and will fight both hummers of their own and other species with equal intensity. However, this behavior may change under certain circumstances.

Recently, the defense tactics of the Blue-throated Hummingbird in an area invaded by both Magnificent and Black-chinned hummingbirds were studied. Although the Blue-throated defended against the Magnificents, it protected its food supply from the smaller Black-chinneds only when the resources were clumped together. When the feeders were separated, the Blue-throated stopped defending against the smaller birds, perhaps because the larger Magnificents were more of a threat to the food supply.

Human beings, cats and much larger birds are also fearlessly attacked, as well as butterflies and insects such as bees, wasps and yellow jackets. Hummingbirds sometimes lose these battles, though, for we have often seen them streaking across summer skies as they are chased by angry yellow jackets. Hummingbirds will usually chase away insects only in their "spare time"—that is, if they are not devoting all their time to defending against other hummers.

A nesting female hummingbird will often establish a temporary territory in the vicinity of her nest that she will defend against interlopers by aerial pursuit. This territory and that of her mate are often different.

Nonnesting females and immature birds of some species are not adept at establishing territories and therefore resort to feeding from floral patches and bushes that have no owner or to poaching on others' territories. In other species, such as the migrant Rufous, females and young can successfully defend territories, even against brightly colored adult males. Another exception is the Fiery-throated Hummingbird, a species in which territorial behavior of the female rivals that of the male, and who is equally adept at holding territories even during the nonbreeding season. As a general rule both males and females of similarly colored species are equally territorial.

In captivity, hummingbirds seem to enjoy engaging in combat with other hummingbirds during the day, only to set their grievances aside at night, when they sleep close to each other, often no more than an inch or so apart.

North American hummingbirds are migratory, with two exceptions. They are the Anna's, which remains in California year-round, and a subspecies of the Allen's, which does not leave its coastline habitat.

The Berylline and Costa's migrate only short distances, while the Ruby-throated and Rufous incredibly travel 2,000 miles or more. Astonishing as it

This male White-eared Hummingbird showed his displeasure at trespassers into his territory by ruffling the feathers of his crown.

may seem, these little birds make their migratory journeys in total solitude, not in safe flocks like some other birds.

Arrival in U.S. breeding grounds begins in February with the Allen's and continues throughout the spring. Then in late August and early September, hummingbirds begin their migratory flights back to the warmer climates of Mexico and Central America, where they winter.

Since flight is so important to a hummingbird, its feathers require a great deal of daily care to keep the plumage in optimum condition.

Bathing is one of hummingbirds' favorite activities. They sometimes bathe on leaves, preferring those that are fresh and green. When bathing on a leaf, a hummingbird will flutter its wings and stroke its head, neck and sides on its wet surface. The little bird will also often drink water from the leaf after its bath.

Hummingbirds also bathe in the rain. From a perched position, they lift and spread their tails and squeeze in and lower their backs, holding their wings close to their sides or lifting them slightly backward. They then will loudly shake their wings and tail feathers and move their heads around to expose the neck to the refreshing mist. The sides of their beaks and heads are cleaned on twigs and branches.

When we first became interested in hummingbirds, we noticed that some would appear to be watching as we watered the garden. We were then amazed to see them flutter down to just-filled planters and dip their lower bodies into the watery pools. Once immersed, they would spread and lift their tails in the water intensely before flying out and shaking water out of their feathers. They also sometimes quickly toss their heads back in order to throw droplets of water on their backs. The first bird to bathe often chases others away, since it seems they prefer to bathe alone.

After a bath, the hummingbird preens and dries its feathers, and those of the wing and tail are carefully groomed with oil from the uropygial gland located near its tail.

After having been caught in a shower, this male Lucifer settles down to preen his wet plumage.

Hummers such as this Ruby-throated and Allen's ruffle all of their feathers from time to time during the day.

In addition, after bathing or feeding, a hummingbird will groom its feathers, feet or beak. Feathers of the head, neck and throat are groomed by the feet, while the bill is used for the remaining plumage. Feathers of the throat are sometimes rubbed against wet leaves or branches.

The front three claws of the hummingbird's foot are very much like a comb and are used to scratch the bird's plumage. The bird bends its head downward in order to put its feathers in reach of the claws.

Hummers can also scratch themselves in midair. This action reaches only the feathers on the front of the body and occurs as the bird descends in a spiral motion toward the ground. The feathers on both the front and back of the body can be scratched in this way.

The comblike claws of the hummingbird's foot are sometimes used for scratching. In this instance, a male Broad-tailed lowers its head to put its gorget within reach.

Wings, tail feathers, back and abdomen are cleaned by the bill. After extending its neck, the bird pokes its bill into the feathers of the breast and abdomen and alternately pulls it up through the plumage. By this motion it is actually rejoining the vanes of each feather with each stroke. While preening, the bird also lifts and spreads its tail and pulls its beak through each of the rectrices.

Beaks are cleaned with the feet. A hummingbird will grasp its bill and scratch it from base to tip in one swift movement. Sometimes the bird's bill is slightly open during this procedure and sometimes it is closed.

At times, after preening, bits of feather and fluff will collect on the bill. These are removed from time to time by the bird with its feet. If the feathery particles get on the tongue, the bird will remove them by extending its tongue and pushing them onto the top of the bill to be scraped away.

An extremely flexible cervical spine enables a hummingbird to contort itself into whatever position necessary for preening hard-to-reach feathers. Note that the wings are being slid through the bills of the first two birds. Male Anna's, Broad-tailed and Ruby-throated hummingbirds.

Bills may also be cleaned by rubbing against twigs or branches, but a bird usually does this after it has stopped feeding for a while. It never cleans its bill with its feet after feeding.

The feet and legs are probably cleaned either by nibbling with the bill or by a licking movement of the tongue.

Hummingbirds also like to take sunbaths. In the early morning, they sometimes position their breasts toward the sun and fluff out their feathers. They extend their necks to expose the feathers of this region to the warm rays and may either spread out or lift and hold up their tails. After a sufficient time under the sun, the bird will luxuriously scratch the warmed areas.

A scrupulous Buff-bellied uses its claws to clean both the inside (LEFT) and outside (RIGHT) of its bill.

These tiny birds also stretch their wings and legs from time to time in what are known as comfort movements. They first stretch each wing to the side and then lower the head and stretch the wings upward. When a bird quickly draws in its legs, it may also be stretching.

There can be no doubt that hummers are inquisitive birds. They are often seen carefully examining red objects of interest (including such unusual items as crimson fingernails and lips!) as they hover. This curiosity is probably due to their never-ending quest for food. They appear to have no fear of human beings; perhaps their confidence in their aerial abilities makes them unafraid.

Nectar, pollen grains and bits of fluff are removed from bills by scraping against twigs. Here a Black-chinned and Buff-bellied engage in this activity, which takes place after every feeding.

Male Anna's stretching.

With eyes closed, this Allen's luxuriously scratches himself after a sunbath.

Hummingbirds do have their share of enemies, though. Leopard frogs and freshwater bass have been known to drag them underwater, and they have been killed by pigeon hawks, kestrels, road runners and orioles. Both the Bat Falcon and the Tiny Hawk are persistent enemies of tropical hummingbirds, as well. In addition, such invertebrates as dragonflies, spiders and praying mantises also prey on them.

The slender, sharp needles of the foxtail grass and purple thistles can become traps for foraging hummingbirds. And fine window screens pose danger, too, for they will often fly into them bill first, only to get stuck and die if not pulled out quickly enough.

Just how does a hummer spend its day? Well, a male Anna's Hummingbird's activities were watched and recorded during a two-day span, with the following results:

Activity	Percentage of time
Feeding from flowers	8.17–8.39
Capturing insects	1.13–1.19
Defending territory	5.94–7.89
Flying for other reasons (includes span when bird was not visible)	2.82–3.48

This hummer spent five or six times as much time perched as it did in the air.

Stiff after a period of prolonged perching, this juvenal Anna's stretches first one wing and then the other.

Its bill loaded with pollen, a male Anna's quenches its thirst from a patch of California fuchsia (ZAUSCHNERIA LATIFOLIA).

Wildflower Pollination | 9

It [the hummingbird] is seen to stop thus some instants before a flower, and dart off like a gleam to another; it visits them all, plunging its little tongue into their bosom, caressing them with its wings, without ever settling, but at the same time never quitting them.

W. C. L. Martin
General History of Humming-Birds
Circa 1840

When looking for hummingbirds in the wild, one rule is to first find the flowers from which they feed, for then you'll find the bird. This is because hummingbirds so often can be found controlling an area that contains one or more flowering plants.

There is a direct relationship between hummingbirds and the flowers they feed from, but in order to appreciate it, it is best to understand the pollination process.

The important flower parts involved in reproduction are the pistil and the stamen. The pistil, composed of the stigma, style and ovary, is the female organ, and the stamen, which is made up of the anther and filament, is the male organ. Within the ovary are ovules, and thousands of minute grains of pollen are found within sacs located inside the anther. Pollen can be either powdery or sticky.

Stamens and pistils do not necessarily mature at the same time. It is not unusual for the anthers to discharge their pollen long before the final ripening of the pistils, or the pistil may mature first.

Other flower parts include the corolla, which is the name given to the petals collectively. It can be polypetalous (with separate petals) or gamopetalous (with "fused" petals). The term "inflorescence" refers to the way that flowers are arranged on the plant.

Pollination takes place when pollen reaches the stigma. There it absorbs water and nutrients and subsequently produces a pollen tube, which reaches an ovule by way of the style. Living cells are brought into the ovule when the

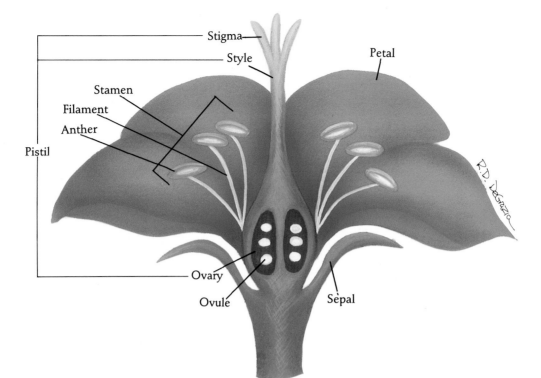

Stigma

Style

Stamen

Filament

Anther

Pistil

Petal

Ovary

Ovule

Sepal

R.D. LeStrac

Hummingbirds help to cross-fertilize flowers with pollen carried on their crowns (BELOW), bills and gorgets (BOTTOM RIGHT). Female Costa's, male Anna's, California fuchsia (ZAUSCHNERIA LATIFOLIA).

pollen tube breaks apart. One of these cells, the sperm, unites with one from the ovary to form a zygote, which will eventually become an embryo enclosed in a seed.

In some plants, pollination occurs when the powdery substance, released into the air and blown about by the wind, lands on the stigma of a flower of its own species. Many trees, herbaceous plants and grasses are pollinated in this way.

Blossoms of "hummingbird flowers" such as the Beard Tongue (PENSTEMON BARBATUS) sometimes have blossoms arranged far apart, permitting the bird to feed without entangling itself. Broad-tailed.

Many "hummingbird flowers" have scarlet stamens (RIBES, TOP) or bracts (CASTILLEJA). Anna's, Black-chinned.

Pollination can also be effected by insects, birds and mammals. Some plants are also capable of self-pollination, which occurs when the pollen of one of its anthers falls directly onto one of the stigmas. In cross-pollination (which results in cross-fertilization), pollen is transferred to the pistil of another flower.

Pollen adheres to the body of an insect or in the case of the hummingbird to its crown, gorget or chin. From there it is transported to other flowers of the same species.

Some flowers that rely on insects and birds for pollination produce a sugary nectar with which to lure and reward them. There are some barren species of flowers, however, which mimic the physical characteristics of nectar-rich hummingbird flowers in order to attract them.

There are certain plants known as hummingbird flowers that attract hummingbirds only. Some are bilaterally symmetrical, their blooms either held horizontally or hanging in pendant fashion in inflorescences that are wide apart, giving the bird plenty of room to feed easily with no danger of entanglement. Many of these unusual blossoms have thick petals, flexible stalks and corollas shaped like trumpets.

Scent is not important to a hummingbird, and many of the flowers from which they feed do not have a fragrance. Since odorless flowers are not attractive to insects, insects do not feed from them. Consequently a good supply of nectar is more likely to be present, and the hummingbird is therefore likely to prefer the odorless flower and thus be an effective pollinator for it. Self-pollination occurs as the hummer feeds from various flowers on a single plant.

Hummingbirds, unlike insects, do not require special floral appendages or surfaces to allow them to land while feeding, and, appropriately, these features are absent in hummingbird flowers.

Also, hummingbird flowers may have long tubular corollas, suitable for hummingbirds but not for bees and other insects that do not have feeding apparatuses long enough to reach the sugary nectar within.

Most of these special flowers that are found in North America are red. They may be completely scarlet, like those in the *Penstemon* genus, or only the stamens (as in *Ribes* and *Aquilegia)* or the bracts (as in *Castilleja)* will be red. And ample supplies of nectar are found at the base of the corolla or in spurs of such flowers as the Columbine *(Aquilegia formosa).* Hummingbird flowers also generally are in bloom during the day.

Approximately 129 species of hummingbird plants exist in the southwestern United States, and about 20 additional flowers have been identified in the Northeast. Some annual herbs and trees can be counted among these plants, but for the most part softwood subshrubs and perennial herbs make up the bulk of them. These flowers also usually have longer blooming periods than those that rely on insects for pollination.

Hummingbirds insert their beaks into the long corollas to harvest the nectar contained within. Sometimes the bill cannot reach far enough to get to the sweet liquid, and the bird will simply extend its tongue. While it drinks, the long reproductive organs of the flower brush against its head or throat and dust them with pollen. Flowers that do not have a typically long corolla, like the Woolly Blue-curl, often have anthers that are especially elongated.

In addition, such flowers as the twinberry and the manzanitas are pollinated by pollen carried on the bill's tip.

Many hummingbird flowers have thick petals, protecting the delicate ovary contained within the flower. In some species there are shallow grooves along the interiors of the petals that guide the beak away from the fragile organs. In some plants, such as those of the *Penstemon* genus, nectar sources are simply situated far from the ovary.

Sometimes a hummingbird (such as this Black-chinned) will tap nectar stored in spurs such as that of the Columbine (AQUILEGIA FORMOSA).

Flowers like the Woolly Blue-curls (TRICHOSTEMA LANATUM) often develop anthers that are especially elongated. Black-chinned.

White-eared feeding from LOESELIA MEXICANA, which has extraordinarily long reproductive organs.

*Black-chinned feeding from Twinberry (*LONICERA INVOLUCRATA*), which is pollinated by pollen carried on the tip of the bird's bill.*

*The delicate ovaries of the Scarlet Penstemon (*PENSTEMON LABROSUS*) are situated far from the nectar supply probed by this Rufous.*

Smaller blossoms are preferred by small hummingbirds, larger blossoms by the larger birds. Some flowers also seem shaped to accommodate the different types of hummingbird bills.

Hummers also drink nectar from flowers that do not require their assistance for pollination, such as the Ocotillo.

Cactus flowers of the tropics and Andes often have flowers that are red and tubular and are pollinated by hummingbirds. In the western United States, however, the Hedgehog Cactus appears to be the only cactus that is fertilized by this tiny bird and not by bees. No one has yet explained the

*Male Costa's feeding from Hedgehog Cactus (*ECHINOCEREUS TRIGLOCHIDIATUS*), which is apparently the only cactus in the western United States pollinated by hummingbirds.*

*A Costa's feeds from the blossoms of the Ocotillo (*FOUQUIERIA SPLENDENS*), a plant that does not rely on the hummingbird for pollination.*

dearth of hummingbird-pollinated cactus in the deserts of this North American region.

It is interesting to note that not all hummingbirds drink nectar by inserting their bills into blossoms and drawing it out. Some species, such as the Purple-crowned Fairy, tap the sweet syrup through punctures the bird makes at the base of the corolla. It squeezes out drops of nectar by pressing its body against the flower. And Guatemalan hummingbirds feed on nectar siphoned from holes in blossoms made by other birds, such as the Cinnamon-bellied Flower Piercer.

There are about 80 species of hummingbird-pollinated flowers in California, 50 in Arizona, 40 in New Mexico, 28 in Oregon, 19 in Colorado, 14 in Idaho, 10 in the southern half of British Columbia and 5 in Alaska.

Powdery pollen, such as that of North American hummingbird flowers, does not stick very well to the smooth beaks of hummingbirds. Yet sometimes a few grains will adhere. Hummers appear to dislike it when grains of pollen remain on their bills after they have fed, and they can often be seen scraping them clean. Some experts believe that the bright substance in their line of vision annoys them and therefore they strive to remove it. Pollen on the bird's plumage is not a problem, since it is not visible to the bird.

Certain species of tropical orchids contain pollinia, or large masses of pollen, which stick *only* to the bird's beak and not very well at all to its feathers. Pollinia of these many species of Andean orchids, fertilized by hummingbirds, is dark brown or blue-gray. It is thought that these dark shades contrast less with the bird's bill and therefore are not so likely to be scraped off, wasting all the potential reproductive cells.

It has further been suggested that the pollen of other orchids which are of various darker shades of white (such as cream or gray-white) are simply in the process of changing or adapting through the mechanism of natural selection, to produce pollen that blends in with the color of the bird's beak.

Hummingbirds vie for nectar with such birds as Flower Piercers or Honey Creepers, which, as their names imply, extract nectar from holes pierced in the flower's base. Butterflies, bees with unusually long tongues and ants also feed from these blossoms. The bees reach the source of nectar by chewing through the thick-fleshed petals, and the resultant holes are used by the ants to go in and out of the nectar reserves.

HUMMINGBIRD FLOWER MITES

In addition, tiny mites have been discovered in hummingbird-pollinated wildflowers. Unlike other mites that are sometimes found on the bird's body or in its nests, these hummingbird flower mites live, mate and reproduce within the flowers from which the bird feeds.

These tiny creatures lay their eggs in or near the flower. It takes from seven to ten days to grow from the larval stage to adulthood. Their diet consists of nectar, although they may also eat pollen substances.

Hummingbird flower mites measure little more than $\frac{1}{2}$ millimeter in length—approximately the size of a period on a printed page—but they can easily be observed within the petals of a flower.

Since most of their life activities take place within or near flowers of a single host plant, a new residence is required when the host dies or flowering ceases. Although they are able to walk the short distances between blossoms of the same inflorescence, they rely on the hummer's frequent trips from flower to flower to transport them to fresh sources of nectar. This journey is made within the confines of the hummingbird's nostrils. Signals within the nasal passages tell the mites when the bird has stopped at a host flower of the right species, for each species of mites resides within the flowers of only certain plant species.

When the bird momentarily stops at a desired bloom, they race down the bill at a speed that has been measured and compared, relative to their size, to that of a cheetah.

Although mites of different species often are transported jointly within the nostrils of a single hummingbird, it is rare for one bird to carry more than a dozen individual mites at a single time.

About 40 species of hummingbird flower mites have been formally named and described, and there are probably hundreds more yet to be uncovered. Nevertheless, it is believed there is probably only one species in North America. Up to 100 individuals of this species *(Rhinoseius epoecus)* can live within the corollas of a single *Castilleja* inflorescence along the California coast. They are carried by the Allen's, Anna's and Rufous hummingbirds.

Within the Western Hemisphere, over 50 species of hummingbirds have so far been discovered carrying hummingbird flower mites that live in over 100 different host plants in an area ranging from California to Chile.

In North America, mites, transported in the nostrils of Rufous Hummingbirds (and Anna's and Allen's), live and reproduce within the corollas of the Castilleja.

NOTE: All families except Agavaceae, Liliaceae and Orchidaceae are dicotyle-donous.

ACANTHACEAE *Anisacanthus thurberi.* Chuparosa, Desert Honeysuckle. Arizona, southwestern New Mexico and northern Mexico.
Beloperone californica. Chuparosa. Deserts of southern California, Arizona and northern Mexico.
Jacobinia ovata. Southern Arizona and northern Mexico.

Female Costa's Hummingbird/ Chuparosa (BELOPERONE CALIFORNICA). *Palm Desert, California.*

Male Lucifer Hummingbird/ Peloncillo Mountains, Century Plant (AGAVE PALMERI). *New Mexico.*

Agave palmeri. Century Plant. New Mexico.

AGAVACEAE   *A. schottii* (♀). Century Plant, Maguey. Southern Arizona to southwestern New Mexico and northern Mexico.
A. utahensis (♀). Century Plant, Maguey. Southeastern California to northern Arizona and southern Utah.

BALSAMACEAE   *Impatiens capensis.* Spotted Touch-Me-Not. Newfoundland and Quebec to Saskatchewan, south to South Carolina, Alabama and Oklahoma.

BIGNONIACEAE   *Campsis radicans.* Trumpet Vine, Trumpet Creeper. New Jersey to Ohio, south to Florida and Texas.

BORAGINACEAE   *Cordia sebestana.* Florida Keys, Everglades and West Indies.

BROMELIACEAE   *Tillandsia balbisiana.* Southern peninsular Florida, West Indies, Mexico, Central and South America.
T. fasciculata. Peninsular Florida, West Indies, Mexico, Central and South America.
T. flexuosa. Southern peninsular Florida, West Indies and South America.

CACTACEAE   *Echinocereus triglochidiatus.* Hedgehog Cactus, Claret Cup Hedgehog. Southeastern California to New Mexico and Colorado, south to northern Mexico.

CAMPANULACEAE   *Lobelia cardinalis.* Cardinal-flower, Scarlet Lobelia. Widespread in the southwest, eastern United States, Mexico and Central America.
L. laxiflora. Southern Arizona to Central America.

Male Ruby-throated Hummingbird/ Trumpet Creeper (BIGNONIACEAE). *Sodus Bay, New York.*

*Male Black-chinned Hummingbird/
Twinberry* (LONICERA
INVOLUCRATA). *California coast.*

CAPRIFOLIACEAE   *Lonicera arizonica.* Honeysuckle. Arizona, New Mexico, Texas and Utah.
L. canadensis. Fly-Honeysuckle. Nova Scotia and eastern Quebec to Saskatchewan, south to Pennsylvania, Ohio, Indiana and Minnesota, and in the mountains of North Carolina.
L. ciliosa. Orange Honeysuckle. Northern California to British Columbia, east to Montana.
L. involucrata ledebourii. Twinberry. California coast.
L. sempervirens. Trumpet Honeysuckle. Connecticut to Florida and west to Oklahoma.

CARYOPHYLLACEAE   *Silene californica.* Indian Pink. Central California to southern Oregon.
S. laciniata. Catchfly. California to western Texas and Mexico.
S. regia. Royal Catchfly. Ohio to eastern Missouri, south to Alabama and Georgia.
S. rotundifolia. Roundleaf Catchfly. West Virginia and southern Ohio to Alabama and Georgia.
S. virginica. Fire Pink. New Jersey and western New York to southern Ontario, south to Georgia and Oklahoma.

CONVOLVULACEAE   *Ipomoea coccinea.* Star-glory, Small Red Morning-glory. Pennsylvania and Rhode Island south to Georgia, west to Illinois, Kansas, Oklahoma, western Texas and Arizona, and south to the tropics.
I. microdactyla. Morning-glory. Extreme southern Florida and the West Indies.

FOUQUIERIACEAE   *Fouquieria splendens.* Ocotillo. Deserts from southeastern California to western Texas, and northern Mexico.

HIPPOCASTANACEAE   *Aesculus pavia* (var. *pavia*). Buckeye. North Carolina to Florida and eastern Texas, and inland to southern Illinois and southern Missouri.

Male Anna's Hummingbird/Indian Pink (SILENE CALIFORNICA). *San Gabriel Mountains, California.*

Female Costa's Hummingbird/ Ocotillo (FOUQUIERIA SPLENDENS). *Palm Desert, California.*

Male Ruby-throated Hummingbird/ Bee-balm (MONARDA IANADENSIS). *Sodus Bay, New York.*

LABIATEAE	*Clinopodium coccineum.* Florida to Georgia and Alabama.

Clinopodium coccineum. Florida to Georgia and Alabama.
Monarda didyma. Bee-balm, Oswego-tea. Minnesota to Michigan, south to New Jersey, West Virginia and Ohio and along the mountains to northern Georgia.
M. fistulosa. Wild Bergamot. Quebec to Manitoba and British Columbia, south to Georgia, Louisiana and Arizona, and west to the Rocky Mountains and California.
M. ianadensis. Bee-balm. New York.
Monardella macrantha. Mountain-pennyroyal. Central California to northern Baja California.
Satureja mimyloides. Mint. Central and southern California.
Salvia henryi. Sage. Southern Arizona to western Texas and Mexico.
S. lemmoni. Sage. Southern Arizona and northern Mexico.
S. spathacea. Pitcher Sage. California Coast Range.
Stachys chamissonis. Hedge-nettle. Coastal California.
S. ciliata. Hedge-nettle. Oregon to British Columbia.
S. coccinea. Hedge-nettle. Southern Arizona to western Texas and Mexico.
Trichostema lanatum. Woolly Blue-curls, Romero. Coast Ranges of central and southern California.

LILIACEAE

Brodiaea ida-maia. Fire-cracker Plant. Northern California to southern Oregon.
B. venusta. Brodiaea. Northwestern California.
Fritillaria recurva. Scarlet Fritillary. Central California to southern Oregon.
Lilum maritimum. Coast Lily. Northern coastal California.
L. parvum. Alpine Lily. Sierra Nevada, California, to southern Oregon.

NYCTAGINACEAE

Allionia coccinea. Southern California, Arizona, New Mexico and northern Mexico.

Male Lucifer Hummingbird/Scarlet Hedge Nettle (STACHYS COCCINEA). New Mexico.

ONAGRACEAE *Zauschneria californica.* California-fuchsia. California to southern Oregon, east to New Mexico, south to northern Mexico.
Z. cana. California-fuchsia. Central and southern California.
Z. garrettii. California-fuchsia. Eastern California to Utah and western Wyoming.
Z. septentrionalis. California-fuchsia. Northern California.

LEGUMINACEAE *Astragalus coccineus.* Locoweed, Rattleweed, Milkvetch. Desert mountains of eastern California, southwestern Arizona and northern Baja California.
Erythrina flabelliformis. Coral-bean, Chilicote. Southern Arizona, southwestern New Mexico, and northern Mexico.
E. herbacea. Coral-tree. Florida to Texas and North Carolina and northeastern Mexico.

LOGANIACEAE *Spigelia marilandica.* Pinkroot, Wormgrass. North Carolina to southern Indiana, southern Missouri and Oklahoma, south to Florida and Texas.

MALVACEAE *Hibiscus coccineus.* Alabama, Georgia and Florida.
Malvaviscus arboreus (var. *drummondii*). Turks-head. Southern Florida to Texas, West Indies and Mexico.

ORCHIDACEAE *Spiranthes orchoides.* Ladies Tresses. Florida, Mexico, Central America, South America and the West Indies.

Male Anna's Hummingbird/
California Fuchsia (ZAUSCHNERIA
CALIFORNIA). *San Gabriel*
Mountains, California.

Female Rufous Hummingbird/Gilia (IPOMOPSIS AGGREATA). *Sierra Mountains, California.*

POLEMONIACEAE   *Collomia rawsoniana.* South-central Sierra Nevada, California.
Gilia splendens (var. *grantii*). Gilia. San Bernardino and San Gabriel Mountains, southern California.
G. subnuda. Gilia. Northern Arizona to Nevada, east to New Mexico and Colorado.
Ipomopsis (Gilia) aggregata. Gilia. Widespread in western North America.
I. arizonica. Gilia. Eastern California to Arizona and Utah.
I. rubra. Gilia. Florida to Texas, Oklahoma and North Carolina.
I. tenuifolia. Gilia. Extreme southern California and northern Baja California.
Polemonium pauciflorum. Polemonium. Southeastern Arizona and northern Mexico and Davis Mountains in Texas.
P. brandegei. Honey Polemonium. Rocky Mountains in Colorado.

RANUNCULACEAE   *Aquilegia canadensis.* Columbine. Nova Scotia to Saskatchewan south to Florida and Texas.
A. desertorum. Columbine. Northern Arizona.
A. elegantula. Rocky Mountain Red Columbine. Arizona and New Mexico, north to southern Utah and Colorado, south to northern Mexico.
A. eximia. Columbine. Coast Range in California.
A. formosa. Columbine. California to Alaska, east to Utah and Montana.
A. shockeyi. Columbine. Desert mountains of eastern California and Nevada.
A. triternata. Columbine. Eastern Arizona to western New Mexico and western Colorado.
Delphinium barbeyi. Subalpine Larkspur. Wyoming to Colorado and Utah.

*Female Costa's Hummingbird/
Scarlet Larkspur* (DELPHINIUM
CARDINALE). *San Gabriel
Mountains, California.*

D. cardinale. Scarlet Larkspur. Central California to Baja California.

D. nelsoni. Low Larkspur, Nelson Larkspur. Idaho to Utah and South Dakota.

D. nudicaule. Larkspur. Central California to southern Oregon.

RUBIACEAE *Bouvardia glaberrima.* Bouvardia. Southern Arizona and New Mexico to northern Mexico.

B. ternifolia. Texas and adjacent New Mexico south to Mexico.

Hamelia patens. Southern peninsular Florida and West Indies.

SAXIFRAGACEAE *Ribes sanguineum.* Red Flowering Currant. California to British Columbia.

Ribes speciosum. Currant, Fuchsia-flowered Gooseberry. Coast from central California to northern Baja California.

SCROPHULARIACEAE *Castilleja affinis.* Paintbrush. California.

C. angustifolia. Paintbrush. Eastern Oregon to southern British Columbia and northwestern Wyoming.

C. applegatei. Paintbrush. Central California to eastern Oregon, east to western Wyoming.

C. austromontana. Paintbrush. Southern Arizona, southern New Mexico and northern Mexico.

C. brevilobata. Paintbrush. Northern California and southern Oregon.

C. breweri. Paintbrush. Sierra Nevada in California.

C. coccinea. Painted-cup, Indian Paintbrush. Massachusetts to Ontario and Manitoba, south to South Carolina, Mississippi and Oklahoma.

C. chromosa. Early Paintbrush. Southern California to eastern Oregon, east to New Mexico, Colorado and Wyoming.

Male Blue-throated Hummingbird/ Smooth Bouvardia (BOUVARDIA GLABERRIMA). *Madera Canyon, Arizona.*

C. covilleana. Paintbrush. Central Idaho and western Montana.

C. crista-galli. Paintbrush. Idaho to western Wyoming.

C. cruenta. Paintbrush. Southeastern Arizona.

C. culbertsonii. Paintbrush. Sierra Nevada in California.

C. elmeri. Paintbrush. Cascade Mountains in Washington.

C. exilis. Paintbrush. Widespread in western North America.

C. foliolosa. Paintbrush. California.

C. franciscana. Paintbrush. Central Coast Range in California.

C. fraterna. Paintbrush. Wallowa Mountains in Oregon.

C. haydeni. Paintbrush. Northern New Mexico to Colorado.

C. hispida. Indian Paintbrush. Oregon to British Columbia, east to Montana.

C. hololeuca. Paintbrush. Channel Islands, California.

C. inconstans. Paintbrush. Northern New Mexico.

C. indivisa. Paintbrush. Southeastern Oklahoma and Texas.

C. integra. Orange Paintbrush. Arizona to western Texas, south to northern Mexico, north to Colorado.

C. lanata. Paintbrush. Arizona and northern Mexico to western Texas.

C. latifolia. Seaside Painted Cup. Monterey coast in California.

C. laxa. Paintbrush. Southern Arizona and northern Mexico.

C. lemmonii. Paintbrush. Sierra Nevada in California.

C. leschkeana. Paintbrush. Point Reyes in California.

C. linariaefolia. Wyoming Paintbrush, Narrow-leaved Paintbrush. California to Oregon, east to New Mexico, Colorado and Wyoming.

C. martinii. Paintbrush. Southern California to Baja California.

C. miniata. Scarlet Paintbrush. Widespread in western North America.

C. minor. Paintbrush. Arizona, New Mexico and northern Mexico.

C. nana. Paintbrush. Sierra Nevada in California.

C. neglecta. Paintbrush. Tiburon peninsula in California.

C. organorum. Paintbrush. Organ Mountains in New Mexico.

C. parviflora. Rosy Paintbrush. California to Alaska and northern Rocky Mountains.

C. patriotica. Paintbrush. Southeastern Arizona and northern Mexico.

C. payneae. Paintbrush. Cascade Mountains from northern California to central Oregon.

C. peirsonii. Paintbrush. Sierra Nevada in California.

C. plagiotoma. Paintbrush. San Gabriel Mountains in California.

C. pruinosa. Paintbrush. Central California to Oregon.

C. rhexifolia. Splitleaf Painted Cup, Rosy Paintbrush. Northern Oregon to British Columbia, east to Colorado and Alberta.

C. roseana. Paintbrush. Coast Range in California.

C. rupicola. Paintbrush. Oregon to British Columbia.

C. sessiliflora. Downy Paintbrush, Plains Paintbrush. Wisconsin and northern Illinois to Saskatchewan and south to Missouri, Texas and Arizona.

C. septentrionalis. Northern Paintbrush, Yellow Paintbrush. Labrador and Newfoundland to Vermont, Michigan, South Dakota and Alberta, south to Colorado and Utah.

C. stenantha. Paintbrush. California.

C. suksdorfii. Paintbrush. Oregon to British Columbia.

C. subincluosa. Paintbrush. Sierra Nevada in California.

C. uliginosa. Paintbrush. Pitkin Marsh in Sonoma County (California).

C. wightii. Paintbrush. Coastline from central California to Washington.

C. wootoni. Paintbrush. White and Sacramento Mountains in New Mexico.

Displacus (Mimulus) aurantiacus. Bush Monkey-flower. California and Oregon.

D. flemingii. Monkey-flower. Channel Islands in California.

D. puniceus. Monkey-flower. Coastal southern California and northern Baja California.

Galvezia speciosa. Islands of southern California and Baja California.

Male Black-chinned Hummingbird/ Crimson Monkey-flower (MIMULUS CARDINALIS). *San Gabriel Mountains, California.*

WILDFLOWER POLLINATION 193

Female Rufous Hummingbird/ Scarlet Penstemon (PENSTEMON BRIDGESII). *San Gabriel Mountains, California.*

Keckia (Penstemon) cordifolia. Beard Tongue. Central California to northern Baja California.

K. corymbosa. Beard Tongue. Northern California.

K. ternata. Southern California and northern Baja California.

Macranthera flammea. Northern Florida to eastern Louisiana and Georgia.

Mimulus cardinalis. Crimson Monkey-flower, Scarlet Monkey-flower. California to Oregon, east to Arizona and Nevada.

M. eastwoodiae. Monkey-flower. Northeastern Arizona and southeastern Utah.

Pedicularis densiflora. Indian Warrior, Lousewort. California to southern Oregon and northern Baja California.

Penstemon barbatus. Penstemon. Arizona to Utah and southern Colorado, and south into Mexico.

P. bridgesii. Scarlet Penstemon. California and Baja California to Colorado and New Mexico.

P. cardinalis. Penstemon. South-central New Mexico, Guadaloupe Mountains in Texas.

P. centranthifolius. Scarlet Bugler. Coast Range in central California to Baja California.

P. clevelandii. Penstemon. Southern California and Baja California.

P. crassulus. Penstemon. Central New Mexico.

P. eatonii. Penstemon. Southern California to Arizona and Utah.

P. labrosus. Scarlet Penstemon. Southern California and northern Baja California.

P. lanceolatus. Penstemon. Southeastern Arizona and southwestern New Mexico, to northern Mexico.

P. newberryi. Mountain Pride. Central California to northern Oregon.

P. parryi. Penstemon. Southern Arizona and northern Mexico.

Male Calliope/Scarlet Penstemon (PENSTEMON LABROSUS). *Mount Pinos, California.*

P. pinifolius. Penstemon. Southeastern Arizona and southwestern New Mexico, to northern Mexico.

P. rupicola. Rock Penstemon. Northern California to Washington.

P. subulatus. Penstemon. Arizona.

P. utahensis. Penstemon. Eastern California to northern Arizona and Utah.

Scrophularia coccinea (= macrantha). Figwort. Southwestern New Mexico.

Female Rufous/Mountain Pride (PENSTEMON NEWBERRYI). *Sierra Nevada Mountains, California.*

Male Violet-crowned Hummingbird/Salvia (SALVIA PURPUREA). *Sinaloa, Mexico.*

Male White-eared Hummingbird/ LOESELIA MEXICANA. *Sinaloa, Mexico.*

Male Buff-bellied Hummingbird/
Fountain plant (RUSSELIA
EQUISETIFORMIS). *Brownsville,*
Texas.

Male Buff-bellied Hummingbird/
Banana plant (MUSA X
PARADISIACA L.). *Brownsville,*
Texas.

Male Magnificent Hummingbird/
Tree Tobacco (NICOTIANA
GLAUCA). *Patagonia, Arizona.*

Male Broad-billed Hummingbird/
Tree Tobacco (NICOTIANA
GLAUCA). *Patagonia, Arizona.*

Male Violet-crowned Hummingbird/Lion's Ears (LEONOTIS NEPETIFOLIA). *Sinaloa, Mexico.*

Male Berylline Hummingbird/ Salvia (CINNA BARINA). *Sinaloa, Mexico.*

Hummingbirds of the World

Doryfera
    johannae — Blue-fronted Lancebill
    ludovicae — Green-fronted Lancebill
Androdon
    aequatorialis — Tooth-billed Hummingbird
Ramphodon
    naevius — Saw-billed Hermit
Glaucis
    dohrnii — Hook-billed Hermit
    aenea — Bronzy Hermit
    hirsuta — Rufous-breasted Hermit
Threnetes
    niger — Sooty Barbthroat
    loehkeni — Bronze-tailed Barbthroat
    leucurus — Pale-tailed Barbthroat
    ruckeri — Band-tailed Barbthroat
Phaethornis
    yaruqui — White-whiskered Hermit
    guy — Green Hermit
    syrmatophorus — Tawny-bellied Hermit
    superciliosus — Long-tailed Hermit
    malaris — Great-billed Hermit
    margarettae — Margaretta Hermit
    eurynome — Scale-throated Hermit
    nigrirostris — Black-billed Hermit

    hispidus — White-bearded Hermit
    anthophilus — Pale-bellied Hermit
    bourcieri — Straight-billed Hermit
    philippii — Needle-billed Hermit
    squalidus — Dusky-throated Hermit
    augusti — Sooty-capped Hermit
    pretrei — Planalto Hermit
    subochraceus — Buff-bellied Hermit
    nattereri — Cinnamon-throated Hermit
    maranhaoensis — Maranhão Hermit
    gounellei — Broad-tipped Hermit
    ruber — Reddish Hermit
    stuarti — White-browed Hermit
    griseogularis — Gray-chinned Hermit
    longuemareus — Little Hermit
    idaliae — Minute Hermit
Eutoxeres
    aquila — White-tipped Sicklebill
    condamini — Buff-tailed Sicklebill
Phaeochroa
    cuvierii — Scaly-breasted Hummingbird
Campylopterus
    curvipennis — Wedge-tailed Sabrewing
    largipennis — Gray-breasted Sabrewing

rufus	Rufous Sabrewing	*Popelairia*	
hyperythrus	Rufous-breasted Sabrewing	*popelairii*	Wire-crested Thorntail
duidae	Buff-breasted Sabrewing	*langsdorffi*	Black-bellied Thorntail
hemileucurus	Violet Sabrewing	*letitiae*	Coppery Thorntail
ensipennis	White-tailed Sabrewing	*conversii*	Green Thorntail
falcatus	Lazuline Sabrewing	*Discosura*	
phainopeplus	Santa Marta Sabrewing	*longicauda*	Racket-tailed Coquette
villaviscensio	Napo Sabrewing	*Chlorestes*	
Eupetomena		*notatus*	Blue-chinned Sapphire
macroura	Swallow-tailed Hummingbird	*Chlorostilbon*	
Florisuga		*mellisugus*	Blue-tailed Emerald
mellivora	White-necked Jacobin	*aureoventris*	Glittering Emerald
Melanotrochilus		*canivetii*	Fork-tailed Emerald
fuscus	Black Jacobin	*ricordii*	Cuban Emerald
Colibri		*swainsonii*	Hispaniolan Emerald
delphinae	Brown Violet-ear	*maugaeus*	Puerto Rican Emerald
thalassinus	Green Violet-ear	*gibsoni*	Red-billed Emerald
coruscans	Sparkling Violet-ear	*russatus*	Coppery Emerald
serrirostris	White-vented Violet-ear	*inexpectatus*	Berlepsch Emerald
Anthracothorax		*stenura*	Narrow-tailed Emerald
viridigula	Green-throated Mango	*alice*	Green-tailed Emerald
prevostii	Green-breasted Mango	*poortmani*	Short-tailed Emerald
nigricollis	Black-throated Mango	*auratus*	Cabanis Emerald
veraguensis	Veraguan Mango	*Cynanthus*	
dominicus	Antillean Mango	*sordidus*	Dusky Hummingbird
viridis	Green Mango	*latirostris*	Broad-billed Hummingbird
mango	Jamaican Mango	*Ptochoptera*	
Avocettula		*iolaima*	Natterer Emerald
recurvirostris	Fiery-tailed Awlbill	*Cyanophaia*	
Eulampis		*bicolor*	Blue-headed Hummingbird
jugularis	Purple-throated Carib	*Thalurania*	
Sericotes		*furcata*	Crowned (Fork-tailed) Woodnymph
holosericeus	Green-throated Carib	*watertonii*	Long-tailed Woodnymph
Chrysolampis		*glaucopis*	Violet-capped Woodnymph
mosquitus	Ruby-topaz Hummingbird	*lerchi*	Lerch Woodnymph
Orthorhyncus		*Augasmall*	
cirstatus	Antillean Crested Hummingbird	*cyaneoberyllina*	Berlioz Woodnymph
Klais		*smaragdinea*	Emerald Woodnymph
guimeti	Violet-headed Hummingbird	*Neolesbia*	
Abeillia		*nehrkorni*	Nehrkorn Hummingbird
abeillei	Emerald-chinned Hummingbird	*Panterpe*	
Stephanoxis		*insignis*	Fiery-throated Hummingbird
lalandi	Black-breasted Plovercrest	*Damophila*	
Lophornis		*julie*	Violet-bellied Hummingbird
ornata	Tufted Coquette	*Lepidopyga*	
gouldii	Dot-eared Coquette	*coeruleogularis*	Sapphire-throated Hummingbird
magnifica	Frilled Coquette	*lilliae*	Sapphire-bellied Hummingbird
delattrei	Rufous-crested Coquette	*goudoti*	Shining-green Hummingbird
stictolopha	Spangled Coquette	*Hylocharis*	
melaniae	Dusky Coquette	*(Basilinna)*	
chalybea	Festive Coquette	*xantusii*	Black-fronted Hummingbird
pavonina	Peacock Coquette	*leucotis*	White-eared Hummingbird
insignibarbis	Bearded Coquette	*(Hylocharis)*	
Paphosia		*eliciae*	Blue-throated Goldentail
helenae	Black-crested Coquette	*sapphirina*	Rufous-throated Sapphire
adorabilis	White-crested Coquette	*cyanus*	White-chinned Sapphire

pyropygia	Flame-rumped Sapphire	
chrysura	Gilded Hummingbird	
(Eucephala)		
grayi	Blue-headed Sapphire	
Chrysuronia		
oenone	Golden-tailed Sapphire	
Goldmania		
violiceps	Violet-capped Hummingbird	
Goethalsia		
bella	Pirre Hummingbird	
Trochilus		
polytmus	Streamertail	
Leucochloris		
albicollis	White-throated Hummingbird	
Polytmus		
guainumbi	White-tailed Goldenthroat	
milleri	Tepui Goldenthroat	
theresiae	Green-tailed Goldenthroat	
Leucippus		
fallax	Buffy Hummingbird	
baeri	Tumbes Hummingbird	
taczanowskii	Spot-throated Hummingbird	
chlorocercus	Olive-spotted Hummingbird	
Taphrospilus		
hypostictus	Many-spotted Hummingbird	
Amazilia		
(Chionogaster)		
chionogaster	White-bellied Hummingbird	
viridicauda	Green-and-white Hummingbird	
(Polyerata)		
candida	White-bellied Emerald	
chionopectus	White-chested Emerald	
versicolor	Versicolored Emerald	
luciae	Honduras Emerald	
fimbriata	Glittering-throated Emerald	
distans	Tachira Emerald	
lactea	Sapphire-spangled Emerald	
amabilis	Blue-chested Hummingbird	
cyaneotincta	Blue-spotted Hummingbird	
rosenbergi	Purple-chested Hummingbird	
boucardi	Mangrove Hummingbird	
franciae	Andean Emerald	
leucogaster	Plain-bellied Emerald	
cyanocephala	Red-billed Azurecrown	
microrhyncha	Small-billed Azurecrown	
(Saucerottia)		
cyanifrons	Indigo-capped Hummingbird	
beryllina	Berylline Hummingbird	
cyanura	Blue-tailed Hummingbird	
saucerrottei	Steely-vented Hummingbird	
tobaci	Copper-rumped Hummingbird	
viridigaster	Green-bellied Hummingbird	
edward	Snowy-breasted Hummingbird	
(Amazilia)		
rutila	Cinnamon Hummingbird	
yucatanensis	Buff-bellied Hummingbird	

tzacatl	Rufous-tailed Hummingbird	
handleyi	Escudo Hummingbird	
castaneiventris	Chestnut-bellied Hummingbird	
amazilia	Amazilia Hummingbird	
viridifrons	Green-fronted Hummingbird	
violiceps	Violet-crowned Hummingbird	
Eupherusa		
poliocerca	White-tailed Hummingbird	
eximia	Stripe-tailed Hummingbird	
cyanophrys	Blue-capped (Oaxaca) Hummingbird	
nigriventris	Black-bellied Hummingbird	
Elvira		
chionura	White-tailed Emerald	
cupreiceps	Coppery-headed Emerald	
Microchera		
albocoronata	Snowcap	
Chalybura		
buffonii	White-vented Plumeleteer	
urochrysia	Bronze-tailed Plumeleteer	
Aphantochroa		
cirrochloris	Sombre Hummingbird	
Lampornis		
clemenciae	Blue-throated Hummingbird	
amethystinus	Amethyst-throated Hummingbird	
viridipallens	Green-throated Mountain-gem	
hemileucus	White-bellied Mountain-gem	
castaneoventris	White-throated (Variable) Mountain-gem	
cinereicauda	Gray-tailed Mountain-gem	
Lamprolaima		
rhami	Garnet-throated Hummingbird	
Adelomyia		
melanogenys	Speckled Hummingbird	
Anthocephala		
floriceps	Blossomcrown	
Urosticte		
benjamini	Whitetip	
Phlogophilus		
hemileucurus	Ecuadorean Piedtail	
harterti	Peruvian Piedtail	
Clytolaema		
rubricauda	Brazilian Ruby	
Polyplancta		
aurescens	Gould Jewelfront	
Heliodoxa		
rubinoides	Fawn-breasted Brilliant	
leadbeateri	Violet-fronted Brilliant	
jacula	Green-crowned Brilliant	
xanthogonys	Velvet-browed Brilliant	
schreibersii	Black-throated Brilliant	
gularis	Pink-throated Brilliant	
branickii	Rufous-webbed Brilliant	
imperatrix	Empress Brilliant	
Eugenes		
fulgens	Magnificent (Rivoli) Hummingbird	
Hylonympha		
macrocerca	Scissor-tailed Hummingbird	

Sternoclyta		
cyanopectus	Violet-chested Hummingbird	
Topaza		
pella	Crimson Topaz	
pyra	Fiery Topaz	
Oreotrochilus		
melanogaster	Black-breasted Hillstar	
estella	Andean Hillstar	
leucopleurus	White-sided Hillstar	
adela	Wedge-tailed Hillstar	
Urochroa		
bougueri	White-tailed Hillstar	
Patagona		
gigas	Giant Hummingbird	
Aglaeactis		
cupripennis	Shining Sunbeam	
aliciae	Purple-backed Sunbeam	
castelnaudii	White-tufted Sunbeam	
pamela	Black-hooded Sunbeam	
Lafresnaya		
lafresnayi	Mountain Velvetbreast	
Pterophanes		
cyanopterus	Great Sapphirewing	
Coeligena		
coeligena	Bronzy Inca	
wilsoni	Brown Inca	
prunellei	Black Inca	
torquata	Collared Inca	
phalerata	White-tailed Starfrontlet	
bonapartei	Golden-bellied Starfrontlet	
orina	Dusky Starfrontlet	
helianthea	Blue-throated Starfrontlet	
lutetiae	Buff-winged Starfrontlet	
violifer	Violet-throated Starfrontlet	
iris	Rainbow Starfrontlet	
Ensifera		
ensifera	Sword-billed Hummingbird	
Sephanoides		
sephanoides	Green-backed Firecrown	
fernandensis	Juan Fernandez Firecrown	
Boissonneaua		
flavescens	Buff-tailed Coronet	
matthewsii	Chestnut-breasted Coronet	
jardini	Velvet-purple Coronet	
Heliangelus		
mavors	Orange-throated Sunangel	
spencei	Merida Sunangel	
amethysticollis	Amethyst-throated Sunangel	
strophianus	Gorgeted Sunangel	
exortis	Tourmaline Sunangel	
viola	Purple-throated Sunangel	
micraster	Little Sunangel	
squamigularis	Olive-throated Sunangel	
speciosa	Green-throated Sunangel	
rothschildi	Rothschild Sunangel	
luminosus	Glistening Sunangel	

Eriocnemis		
nigrivestis	Black-breasted Puffleg	
soderstromi	Söderström Puffleg	
vestitus	Glowing Puffleg	
godini	Turquoise-throated Puffleg	
cupreoventris	Coppery-bellied Puffleg	
luciani	Sapphire-vented Puffleg	
isaacsonii	Isaacson Puffleg	
mosquera	Golden-breasted Puffleg	
glaucopoides	Blue-capped Puffleg	
mirabilis	Colorful Puffleg	
alinae	Emerald-bellied Puffleg	
derbyi	Black-thighed Puffleg	
Haplophaedia		
aureliae	Greenish Puffleg	
lugens	Hoary Puffleg	
Ocreatus		
underwoodii	Booted Racket-tail	
Lesbia		
victoriae	Black-tailed Trainbearer	
nuna	Green-tailed Trainbearer	
Sappho		
sparganura	Red-tailed Comet	
Polyonymus		
caroli	Bronze-tailed Comet	
Zodalia		
glyceria	Purple-tailed Comet	
Ramphomicron		
microrhynchum	Purple-backed Thornbill	
dorsale	Black-backed Thornbill	
Metallura		
phoebe	Black Metaltail	
theresiae	Coppery Metaltail	
purpureicauda	Purple-tailed Thornbill	
aeneocauda	Scaled Metaltail	
baroni	Violet-throated Metaltail	
eupogon	Fire-throated Metaltail	
williami	Viridian Metaltail	
tyrianthina	Tyrian Metaltail	
iracunda	Perija Metaltail	
Chalcostigma		
ruficeps	Rufous-capped Thornbill	
olivaceum	Olivaceous Thornbill	
stanleyi	Blue-mantled Thornbill	
heteropogon	Bronze-tailed Thornbill	
herrani	Rainbow-bearded Thornbill	
Oxypogon		
guerinii	Bearded Helmetcrest	
Opisthoprora		
euryptera	Mountain Avocetbill	
Taphrolesbia		
griseiventris	Gray-bellied Comet	
Aglaiocercus		
kingi	Long-tailed Sylph	
coelestis	Violet-tailed Sylph	

Oreonympha	
nobilis	Bearded Mountaineer
Augastes	
scutatus	Hyacinth Visorbearer
lumachellus	Hooded Visorbearer
Schistes	
geoffroyi	Wedge-billed Hummingbird
Heliothryx	
barroti	Purple-crowned Fairy
aurita	Black-eared Fairy
Heliactin	
cornuta	Horned Sungem
Loddigesia	
mirabilis	Marvellous Spatuletail
Heliomaster	
constantii	Plain-capped Starthroat
longirostris	Long-billed Starthroat
squamosus	Stripe-breasted Starthroat
furcifer	Blue-tufted Starthroat
Rhodopis	
vesper	Oasis Hummingbird
Thaumastura	
cora	Peruvian Sheartail
Philodice	
evelynae	Bahama Woodstar
bryantae	Magenta-throated Woodstar
mitchellii	Purple-throated Woodstar
Doricha	
enicura	Slender Sheartail
eliza	Mexican Sheartail
Tilmatura	
dupontii	Sparkling-tailed (Dupont) Hummingbird
Microstilbon	
burmeisteri	Slender-tailed Woodstar
Calothorax	
lucifer	Lucifer Hummingbird
pulcher	Beautiful Hummingbird
Archilochus	
colubris	Ruby-throated Hummingbird

alexandri	Black-chinned Hummingbird
Calliphlox	
amethystina	Amethyst Woodstar
Mellisuga	
minima	Vervain Hummingbird
Calypte	
anna	Anna's Hummingbird
costae	Costa's Hummingbird
helenae	Bee Hummingbird
Stellula	
calliope	Calliope Hummingbird
Atthis	
heloisa	Bumblebee Hummingbird
ellioti	Wine-throated Hummingbird
Myrtis	
fanny	Purple-collared Woodstar
Eulidia	
yarrellii	Chilean Woodstar
Myrmia	
micrura	Short-tailed Woodstar
Acestrura	
mulsant	White-bellied Woodstar
decorata	Decorated Woodstar
bombus	Little Woodstar
heliodor	Gorgeted Woodstar
berlepschi	Esmeralda Woodstar
harterti	Hartert Woodstar
Chaetocercus	
jourdanii	Rufous-shafted Woodstar
Selasphorus	
platycercus	Broad-tailed Hummingbird
rufus	Rufous Hummingbird
sasin	Allen's Hummingbird
flammula	Volcano (Rose-throated) Hummingbird
torridus	Heliotrope-throated Hummingbird
simoni	Cerise-throated Hummingbird
ardens	Glow-throated Hummingbird
scintilla	Scintillant Hummingbird

Bibliography

Aldrich, E. C. 1945. Nesting of the Allen Hummingbird. *Condor* 47(4):137–48.

———. 1956. Pterylography and molt of the Allen Hummingbird. *Condor* 58:121–33.

Armstrong, N. J. 1974. *A Collector's History of Fans.* Potter, New York.

———. 1978. *The Book of Fans.* Mayflower Books, New York.

Aymar, G. C. 1935. *Bird Flight.* Dodd, New York.

Baker, H. G. 1975. Sugar concentrations in nectars from hummingbird flowers. *Biotropica* 7(1):37–41.

Banks, R. C., and D. R. Medina. 1963. An albinistic Anna Hummingbird. *Condor* 65:69–70.

Bartholomew, G. A., T. R. Howell and T. J. Cade. 1957. Torpidity in the White-throated Swift, Anna Hummingbird, and Poor-will. *Condor* 59:145–55.

Beebe, C. W. 1906. *The Bird: Its Form and Function,* Holt, New York.

Bene, F. 1945. The role of learning in the feeding behavior of Black-chinned Hummingbirds. *Condor* 47(1):3–21.

Bent, A. C. 1964. *Life Histories of North American Cuckoos, Goatsuckers, Hummingbirds and Their Allies.* Dover Publications, New York.

Beuchat, C. A., S. B. Chaplin and M. L. Morton. 1979. Ambient temperature and the daily energetics of two species of hummingbirds, *Calypte anna* and *Selasphorus rufus. Physiol. Zool.* 52(3):280–95.

Blake, C. H. 1939. The flight of hummingbirds. *New England Naturalist* 3:1–5.

Bradfield, M. 1974. Birds of the Hopi region, their Hopi names, and notes on their ecology. *Museum of Northern Arizona Bulletin* No. 48.

Brown, J. H., A. Kodric-Brown, T. G. Whitham and H. W. Bond. 1981. *Southwestern Naturalist* 26 (2):133–45.

Burland, C., 1965. *North American Mythology.* Paul Hamlyn, London.

Calder, W. A. 1971. Temperature relationships and nesting of the Calliope Hummingbird. *Condor* 73:314–21.

———. 1972. Piracy of nesting materials from and by the Broad-tailed Hummingbird. *Condor* 74(4):485.

———. 1974. Thermal and radiant environment of a winter hummingbird nest. *Condor* 76:268–73.

Carpenter, F. L. 1974. Torpor in an Andean hummingbird: its ecological significance. *Science* 183:545–47.

Chandra-Bose, D. A., and J. C. George. 1964. Studies on the structure and physiology of the flight muscles of birds. *Pavo* 2(2):111–14.

Clyde, D. P. 1972. Anna's Hummingbird in adult male plumage feeds nestling. *Condor* 74:102.

Cogswell, H. L. 1949. Alternate care of two nests in the Black-chinned Hummingbird. *Condor* 51:176–78.

Collins, C. T. 1978. The natal pterylosis of hummingbirds. *Bull. Southern California Acad. Sci.* 77(1):14–21.

Colton, H. S. 1949. *Hopi Kachina Dolls.* University of New Mexico, Albuquerque.

Colwell, R. K. 1973. Competition and coexistence in a simple tropical community. *American Naturalist* 107(958):737–60.

————, B. J. Betts, P. Bunnell, F. L. Carpenter and P. Feinsinger. 1974. Competition for the nectar of *Centropogon valerii* by the hummingbird *Colibri thalassinus* and the flower-piercer *Diglossa plumbea,* and its evolutionary implications. *Condor* 76:447–84.

————, and S. Naeem, 1979. The first known species of hummingbird mite north of Mexico: *Rhinoseius epoecus* n.sp. *Entomological Society of America* 72(4):485–90.

Conway, W. G. 1961. Hummingbirds with wrinkles. *Animal Kingdom* 65(4):151–54.

Cooke, M. T. 1937. Flight speed of birds. U.S. Dept. of Agriculture Circular No. 428:1–13.

Copenhaver, C., and P. W. Ewald. 1980. Cost of territory establishment in hummingbirds. *Oecologia* 46:155–60.

Courlander, H. 1971. *The Fourth World of the Hopis.* Crown, New York.

Craigie, E. H. 1928. Observations on the brain of the hummingbird. *Journal of Comparative Neurology* 45(2):377–481.

Curtin, J. 1903. *Creation Myths of Primitive America in Relation to the Religious History and Mental Development of Mankind.* Little, Brown, and Company, Boston.

Curtis, E. W. 1926. *The North American Indian.* Johnson Reprint Corporation, New York.

————. 1927. *The North American Indian.* Johnson Reprint Corporation, New York.

Darling, L., and L. Darling.1962. *Bird.* Houghton Mifflin Company, Boston.

DeBenedictis, P. A., F. B. Gill, F. R. Hainsworth, G. H. Pyke and L. L. Wolf. 1978. Optimal meal size in hummingbird. *American Naturalist* 112(984):301–16.

Delacour, J. 1926. Humming Birds. *Avicultural Magazine* 4(2):2–29.

Doughty, R. W. 1975. *Feather Fashions and Bird Preservation.* University of California Press, Berkeley.

Dressler, R. L. 1971. Dark pollinia in hummingbird-pollinated orchids or do hummingbirds suffer from strabismus? *American Naturalist* 105(941):80–83.

Epting, R. J., and T. M. Casey. 1973. Power output and wing disc loading in hovering hummingbirds. *American Naturalist* 107(958):761–65.

Ewald, P. W. 1979. The hummingbird and the calorie. *Natural History* 88(7):93–98.

Feinsinger, P., and S. B. Chaplin. 1975. On the relationship between wing disc loading and foraging strategy in hummingbirds. *American Naturalist* 109(966):217–24.

Feldman, S. 1965. *The Storytelling Stone.* Dell Publishing Company, New York.

French, N. R. 1959. Torpidity in cave-roosting hummingbirds. *Condor* 61(3):223.

Gass, C. L., and K. P. Lertzman. 1980. Capricious mountain weather: a driving variable in hummingbird territorial dynamics. *Canadian Journal of Zoology* 58:1,964–68.

Gifford, E. W., and G. H. Block, 1930. *California Indian Nights Entertainments.* Arthur H. Clark Company, Glendale, Calif.

Glenny, F. H. 1954. Deletion of the systemic arches and evolution of the aortic arch system in birds. *Ohio Journal of Science* 54(4):240.

Gould, J. 1861. *Humming-Birds.* Taylor, London.

Grant, J. 1959. Hummingbirds attacked by wasps. *Canadian Field-Naturalist* 73:174.

Grant, K. A., and V. Grant. 1968. *Hummingbirds and Their Flowers,* Columbia University Press, New York.

Grant, V., and K. A. Grant. 1979. The pollination spectrum in the southwestern American cactus flora. *Plant Systematics and Evolution* 133:29–37.

Greenwalt, C. H. 1960. *Hummingbirds.* Doubleday & Company, Garden City, N.Y.

————. W. Brandt and D. D. Friel. 1960. Iridescent colors of hummingbird feathers. *Journal of the Optical Society of America,* 50(10):1005–13.

————. 1960. The iridescent colors of hummingbird feathers. *Proceedings of the American Philosophical Society* 104(3): 249–53.

Grinyer, I., and J. C. George. 1969. Some observations on the ultrastructure of the hummingbird pectoral muscles. *Canadian Journal of Zoology* 47: 771–74.

Hainsworth, F. R. 1973. On the tongue of a hummingbird: its role in the rate and energetics of feeding. *Comp. Biochem. Physiol. A. Comp. Physiol.* 46(1):65–78.

————.1974. Food quality and foraging efficiency—the efficiency of sugar assimilation by hummingbirds. *J. Comp. Physiol.* 88:425–31.

————. 1981. Energy regulation in hummingbirds. *American Scientist* 69:420–29.

————, B. G. Collins and L. L. Wolf. 1978. The function of torpor in hummingbirds. *Physiol. Zool.* 50(3):215–22.

————, and L. L. Wolf. 1970. Regulation of oxygen consumption and body temperature during torpor in a hummingbird *Eulampis jugularis. Science* 168:368–69.

————. 1972. Crop volume, nectar concentration and hummingbird energetics. *Comp. Biochem. Physiol.* 42A:359–66.

————. 1976. Nectar characteristics and food selection by hummingbirds. *Oecologia* 25:101–13.

Hamilton, W. J., III. 1965. Sun-oriented display of the Anna's Hummingbird. *The Wilson Bulletin* 77(1):38–44.

Harrington, J. P. 1932. *Karuk Indian Myths.* U.S. Government Printing Office, Washington, D.C.

Hartman, F. A. 1954. Cardiac pectoral muscles of trochilids. *Auk* 71:467–69.

————, and K. A. Brownell. 1959. Liver lipids in hummingbirds. *Condor* 61(4):270–77.

Heinroth, O., and K. Heinroth. 1958. *The Birds.* University of Michigan Press, Ann Arbor.

Herling, L. 1947. Courtship and mating of Broad-tailed Hummingbird in Colorado. *Condor* 49:126.

Horvath, O. H. 1964. Seasonal differences in Rufous Hummingbird nest height and their relation to nest climate. *Ecology* 45(2):235–41.

Houghton, G. 1966. Hummingbird hovering, an aero-biophysical phenomenon. *Proceedings of the American Philosophical Society* 110(3):165–73.

Howell, T. R., and W. R. Dawson, 1954. Nest temperatures and attentiveness in the Anna Hummingbird. *Condor* 56:93–97.

Inouye, D. W. 1975. Why don't more hummingbird-pollinated flowers have dark-colored pollen? *American Naturalist* 109(967):377–78.

Janzen, D. H. 1983. *Costa Rican Natural History.* University of Chicago Press, Chicago.

Jardine, W. n.d. *Ornithology. Humming Birds.* Chatto, London.

Jewett, P. H., J. R. Sommer and E. A. Johnson. 1971. Cardiac muscle. *Journal of Cell Biology* 49(1):50–65.

Johnsgard, P. A. 1983. *The Hummingbirds of North America.* Smithsonian Institution Press, Washington, D.C.

Jones, J. A. 1829. *Tales of an Indian Camp.* Henry Colburn and Richard Bentley, London.

Kelly, J. W. 1955. History of the nesting of an Anna Hummingbird. *Condor* 57:347–53.

Koester, F., and H. Stoewesand. 1973. Schildlaeuse als Honigtau für Kolibris und Insekten. *Bonn. Zool. Beitr.* 24($\frac{1}{2}$):15–23.

Kuban, J. F., and R. L. Neill. 1980. Feeding ecology of hummingbirds in the highlands of the Chisos Mountains, Texas. 82:180–85.

Langner, S. 1973. Zur biologie des Hochlandkolibris *Oreotrochilus estella* in den Anden Boliviens. *Bonn. Zool. Beitr.* 24($\frac{1}{2}$):24–47.

Lanyon, W. E. 1963. *Biology of Birds.* Natural History Press, Garden City, N.Y.

Lasiewski, R. C. 1964. Body temperatures, heart and breathing rate, and evaporative water loss in hummingbirds. *Physiol. Zool.* 37(2):212–23.

————. 1964. Oxygen consumption of torpid, resting, active and flying humming-birds. *Physiol. Zool.* 36(2):122–40.

————, and R. J. Lasiewski. 1967. Physiological responses of the Blue-throated and Rivoli's hummingbirds. *Auk* 84:34–48.

Lester, K. M. 1940. *Illustrated History of Those Frills and Furbelows of Fashion Which Have Come to be Known as Accessories of Dress.* Manual Arts Press, Peoria, Ill.

Lockett, H. G. 1933. The unwritten literature of the Hopi. *University of Arizona Bulletin* 4(4).

Martin, W.C.L. n.d. *General History of Humming-Birds or the Trochilidae.* Chatto, London.

Miller, R. S., and R. E. Miller. 1971. Feeding activity and color preference of Ruby-throated Hummingbirds. *Condor* 73:309–13.

Mirsky, E. N. 1976. Song divergence in hummingbird and junco populations on Guadalupe Island. *Condor* 78:230–35.

Monroe, M. 1957. Hummingbird killed by frog. *Condor* 59(1):69.

Morony, J. J., Jr., W. J. Bock and J. J. Ferrand. 1975. *Reference List of the Birds of the World.* American Museum of Natural History, New York.

Nickell, W. P. 1948. Alternate care of two nests by a Ruby-throated Hummingbird. *The Wilson Bulletin* 60(4):242–43.

————. 1956. Bird and insect guests at a sapsucker tree. *Jackpine Warbler* 34(3):117.

Norris, R. A., C. E. Connell and D. W. Johnston. 1957. Notes on fall plumages, weights, and fat condition in the Ruby-throated Hummingbird. *The Wilson Bulletin* 69(2):155–63.

Olden, S. E. 1923. *Karoc Indian Stories.* Harr Wagner Publishing Co., San Francisco.

Orr, R. T. 1939. Observations on the nesting of the Allen Hummingbird. *Condor* 41:17–24.

Ortiz-Crespo, F. I. 1972. A new method to separate immature and adult hummingbirds. *Auk* 89:851–57.

Pasquier, R. F. 1977. *Watching Birds: An Introduction to Ornithology.* Houghton Mifflin Company, Boston.

Pearson, O. P. 1950. The metabolism of hummingbirds. *Condor* 52(4):145–52.

————. 1953. Use of caves by hummingbirds and other species at high altitudes in Peru. *Condor* 55:17–20.

————. 1960. Speed of the Allen Hummingbird while diving. *Condor* 62(5):403.

Percival, M. 1921. *The Fan Book.* Frederick A. Stokes Co., New York.

Peterson, R. T. 1961. *A Field Guide to Western Birds.* Houghton Mifflin Company, Boston.

————, and E. L. Chalif. 1973. *A Field Guide to Mexican Birds.* Houghton Mifflin Company, Boston.

Pettingill, O. S., Jr. 1956. *A Laboratory and Field Manual of Ornithology.* Burgess Publishing Company, Minneapolis.

Pitelka, F. A. 1942. Territoriality and related problems in North American hummingbirds. *Condor* 44:189–204.

————. 1951. Ecologic overlap and interspecific strife in breeding populations of Anna and Allen hummingbirds. *Ecology* 32(4):641–61.

Poley, D. 1971. Körperpflege der Kolibris. *Bonn. Zool. Beitr.* 22(^{3}/$_4$):236–46.

Poley, V. D. 1968. Beitrag zum Balzverhalten der Kolibris. *J. Orn.* 109:37–42.

Rand, A. L. 1967. *Ornithology: An Introduction.* W. W. Norton & Company, New York.

Reichholf, H., and J. Reichholf. 1973. Honigtau der Bracaatinga-Schildaus als Winternahrung von Kolibris. *Bonn. Zool. Beitr.* 24(^{1}/$_2$):7–14.

Riba, R., and T. Herrera. 1973. Ferns, lichens, and hummingbird's nests. *American Fern Journal* 63(3):128.

Ridgway, R. 1890. The humming birds. *Report of the U.S. National Museum for 1890,* pp. 253–383.

Robbins, C. S., B. Bruun and H. S. Zim. 1966. *Birds of North America.* Golden Press, New York.

Savile, D.B.O. 1957. Adaptive evolution in the avian wing. *Evolution* 11:212–24.

Scheithauer, W. 1967. *Hummingbirds.* Thomas Y. Crowell, New York.

Skutch, A. F. 1973. *The Life of the Hummingbird.* Crown, New York.

Smith, A. 1926. Fruit-eating hummingbirds. *Condor* 28:243.

Smith, W. K., S. W. Roberts and P. C. Miller. 1974. Calculating the nocturnal energy expenditure of an incubating Anna's Hummingbird. *Condor* 76:176–83.

Southwick, E. E., and A. K. Southwick. 1980. Energetics of feeding on tree sap by Ruby-throated Hummingbirds in Michigan. *American Midland Naturalist* 104(2):328–34.

Squire, G. 1974. *Dress and Society.* Viking Press, New York.

Stiles, F. G. 1971. Time, energy, and territoriality of the Anna Hummingbird (*Calypte anna*). *Science* 173:818–21.

———. 1978. Possible specialization for hummingbird-hunting in the tiny hawk. *Auk* 95:550–53.

———. 1982. Aggressive and courtship displays of the male Anna's Hummingbird. *Condor* 84:208–25.

Strong, C. L. 1960. Does a hummingbird find its way to nectar through its sense of smell? *Scientific American* 202(2):157–66.

Storer, J. H. 1948. *The Flight of Birds.* Cranbrook Institute of Science, Bloomfield Hills, Mich.

Thielcke, G. A. 1976. *Bird Sounds.* University of Michigan Press, Ann Arbor.

Trousdale, B. 1954. Copulation of Anna Hummingbirds. *Condor* 56:110.

Van Riper, W. 1958. Hummingbird feeding preferences. *Auk* 75:100–101.

Verbeek, N.A.M. 1971. Hummingbirds feeding on sand. *Condor* 73(1):112–13.

Voth, H. R. 1905. *The Traditions of the Hopi.* Field Columbian Museum, No. 96.

Wagner, H. O. 1948. Die Balz des Kolibris *Selasphorus platycercus. Zool. Jahrb. Abt. Syst. Oekol. Geogr. Tiere.* 77:267–78.

———. 1954. Versuch einer Analyse der Kolibribalz. *Z. Tierpsychol.* 11:182–212.

———. 1955. The molt of hummingbirds. *Auk* 72:286–91.

Wallace, G. J. 1975. *An Introduction to Ornithology.* Macmillan Company, New York.

Walls, G. L. 1963. *The Vertebrate Eye and Its Adaptive Radiation.* Hafner Publishing Company, New York.

Weydemeyer, W. 1927. Notes on the location and construction of the nest of the Calliope Hummingbird. *Condor* 29:19–24.

Weis-Fogh, T. 1972. Energetics of hovering flight in hummingbirds and in Drosophila. *J. Exp. Biol.* 56:79–104.

Wells, S., and L. F. Baptista. 1979. Displays and morphology of an Anna X Allen hummingbird hybrid. *The Wilson Bulletin* 91(4):524–32.

Weymouth, R. D., R. C. Lasiewski and A. J. Berger. 1964. The tongue apparatus in hummingbirds. *Acta. Anat.* 58:252–70.

Wheeler, T. G. 1980. Experiments in feeding behavior of the Anna Hummingbird. *The Wilson Bulletin* 92(1):53–62.

Wiegert, R. 1959. Rufous Hummingbird feeding on sap of English walnut at sapsucker holes. *Auk* 76:526–27.

Williamson, F.S.L. 1956. The molt and testis cycles of the Anna Hummingbird. *Condor* 58(5):342–66.

Wolf, L. L., and F. R. Hainsworth. 1971. Time and energy budgets of territorial hummingbirds. *Ecology* 52(6):980–88.

———. 1972. Environmental influence on regulated body temperature in torpid hummingbirds. *Comp. Biochem. Physiol.* 41A:167–73.

———. 1975. Foraging efficiencies and time budgets in nectar-feeding birds. *Ecology* 56:117–28.

———. 1977. Temporal patterning of feeding by hummingbirds. *Animal Behavior* 25:976–89.

Wright, Barton. 1973. *Kachinas: A Hopi Artist's Documentary.* Northland Press, Flagstaff, Ariz., and the Heard Museum, Phoenix.

Wright, B. S. 1979. Baltimore Oriole kills hummingbird. *Auk* 79(1):112.

Index

NOTE: page numbers in *italics* refer to illustrations

Adrenals, 46
Aggressive behavior, 152, *153–60,* 154
Air sacs, 50, 52
Albino hummingbirds, 67
Allen's Hummingbird, *6,* 7, *7,* 60, *62, 63,*
    79, 90, 99, 103, *103,* 120, 161, *164,*
    170, 183
  nests, 105, *106,* 111
  pterylography of, *61*
American Indians, 2, 60, *61*
Anatomy, 39–57
Andean Hillstar Hummingbird, 143
Anna's Hummingbird, *8,* 9, *9, 51, 58,*
    64, 65, *67, 68, 92, 95, 100,* 101, *112,*
    116, *134, 136,* 137, 138, 140, 141,
    143, *143, 149,* 161, *166, 170–72,*
    174, 176, 183, *187, 189*
  daily activities, 170
  displays, 103–4, *103, 104*
  molting cycle, 75, *75–78, 78*
  nestlings, 114, 120–21, *120–31*
  nests, 105, *106,* 111
  songs of, 151, 152
Antillean Crested Hummingbird, 5
Arawaks, 2
Arenas (leks), 104–5
Argyle, Duke of, 2

Assimilation of food, 138–39
Autonomic nervous system, 48
Aztecs, 2

Bahama Woodstar Hummingbird, 5
Bathing, 163
Beaks, 166
Berylline Hummingbird, *10,* 11, *11,* 39,
    161, *199*
Bills, *39,* 39–40, *40,* 152, *154,* 166, 168,
    168, 169
Black-chinned Hummingbird, *12,* 13,
    13, 67, 67, 72–73, 96, 103, *107, 117,*
    119, 120, 140, 148, 161, *169, 176,*
    178–80, 186, 193
Blood, 40
Blue-chested Hummingbird, 152
Blue-throated Hummingbird, *14,* 15, *15,*
    50, 67, 70, *71,* 99, 120, 135, *144–45,*
    148, 161, *191*
Bones, 52–53, 63
Boucard, Adolphe, 59–60
Brain, 47
Breeding behavior, 101. *See also*
    Courtship
Breeding season, 101–2
Broad-billed Hummingbird, *16,* 17, *17,*
    69, 74, 82, 146, 198
Broad-tailed Hummingbird, *18,* 19, *19,*

39, *65, 91,* 103, 116, *132, 147, 165,*
  167, 175
Bronchi, 50
Brooding, 114, 116
Buff-bellied Hummingbird, *20,* 21, *21,*
  65, *168, 169, 197*
Bumblebee Hummingbird, 5

Cactus flowers, 180, *181,* 182
Calliope Hummingbird, *22,* 23, *23, 93,*
  103, 111, 114, *195*
Calories, expenditures of, 136, 138
Cerebellum, 47–48
Cerebral cortex, 48
Chicks. *See* Nestlings
Circulatory system, 40–41
Claws, 165, *165*
Clutch, 111, 113
Coloration, 65–69
Comfort movements, 169
Contour feathers, 63
Cooling system, evaporative, 52
Copulation, 48, 104, 105
Costa's Hummingbird, *xii, 24,* 25, *25,*
  65, *67, 80, 98,* 103, *107, 108, 110,*
  151, 161, *174, 181, 184, 187, 191*
  nestlings, *115–19*
Courtship, 102, 152. *See also* Display
Crop, 42
Cuban "Bee" Hummingbird, 1
Cuban Emerald Hummingbird, 5
Curiosity, 169

Diet, 134–35
Digestive system, *41,* 41–42
Display, 102–5, *103, 104*
Down feathers, 62–63
Duck Hawk, 99

Eggs, 111, 113, 116
Egg tooth, 113
Endocrine glands, 45–46
Evaporative cooling system, 52
Eyes, *43,* 43–45

Fat, storage of, 141
Feathers, 59–78, 163, 165. *See also* Skins
  colors of, 65–69
  contour, 63
  down, 62–63
  molting, *67,* 70, 71, 75, 78
  number of, 60
  parts of, 60
  purposes of, 60
  rectrices (tail), 64–65
  remiges (flight), 63
Feather tracts (pterylae), 60, 62
Feeders, 135, 140
Feeding, 133–36, 138–41
Feet, 53, 87, 168
Fiery-throated Hummingbird, 161
Flight, 1–2, 85–99
  backward, 91, *92*
  beating of wings in, 96–98
  of birds in general, 85–87
  display, 102–3, *103, 104*
  of fledglings, 119

hovering, 92–96, *94, 95, 136, 139,* 141
lift off, 87
speed of, 98–99
territorial hummingbirds and, 140
upside down, 92
Flight feathers (remiges), 63
Flower mites, 182–83, *183*
Flowers, 135, 138–40, 184–99, *184–99*
  pollination of, 173, *174–76, 175,* 177,
    178–81, 180, 182
Food, 138–39
Foraging, 140–41

Garnet-throated Hummingbird, 148
Gizzard, 42
Glandular system, 45–46
Gllittering-throated Emerald
    Hummingbird, 63
Glottis, 49
Gonads, 45–46, 48, 101
Green Violet-ear Hummingbird, 5
Grew, Nehemiah, 1, 101
Grooming, 163, 165–66

Habitats, 3
Hatching, 113
Heart, 40–41
  during torpidity, 148
Hill, R., 109
Hopi, 2
Hormones, 45, 46
Hovering, 92–96, *94, 95, 136,* 138, 141

Incubation, *112,* 113, 114
Insects, 135, 141
Intestines, 42
Iridescent coloration, 66–69

Kidneys, 56

Large intestine, 42
Larynx, 49–50, 57
Leclerc, George Louis, 59
Legends and myths, hummingbirds in,
    2–3
Legs, 168
Leks (arenas), 104–5
Lesson, René-Primever, 66
Life expectancy, 148
Liver, 42
Long-tailed Sylphs, 99
Lucifer Hummingbird, *26,* 27, *27, 39,* 65,
    146, 158–60, 163, 184, 188
Lungs, 49, 50
Lymphatic system, 41

Magnificent (Rivoli) Hummingbird, *28,*
    29, 29, 42, *51, 97,* 148, 161, *198*
Martin, W.C.L., 173
Metabolism, 133–35, 141. *See also*
    Torpor
Mexico, 2
Migration, 161, 163
Mites, flower, 182–83, *183*
Mockingbird, 97
Molting, *67,* 70, *70,* 71, 75, 78, 143
Muscular system, 46–47

Myths and legends, hummingbirds in, 2–3

Names of hummingbirds, 3
Nectar, 134, 135, *135,* 138, 139, 141, 177, 180
Neossoptiles (down feathers), 62–63
Nervous system, 47–48
Nestlings, 62, *62,* 63, 113–16, *115–31*
Nests, 105, *106–10,* 108–9, 111, 114, 120, 161
Newton, Isaac, 66
Nictitating membrane, *44,* 45

Ovaries, 48
Oxygen consumption, 141, 148

Pancreas, 42
Pancreatic islets, 45
Parabronchi, 50
Parasympathetic nervous system, 48
Parathyroids, 45
Pipping, 113
Pituitary gland, 45
Plain-capped Starthroat Hummingbird, 5
Pollen, 182
Pollination, 173, *174–76,* 175, 177, *178–81,* 180, 182
Predators, 170
Preening, 163, 166, *166–67*
Pterylae (feather tracts), 60, 62
Pterylosis, 60
Purple-backed Thorn-billed Hummingbird, 39
Purple-crowned Fairy Hummingbird, 182
Purple-throated Carib Hummingbird, 148
Purple-throated Mountain-gem Hummingbird, 152

Rectrices (tail feathers), 64–65
Red-billed Azurecrown Hummingbird, 71
Remiges (flight feathers), 63
Reproductive system, 48–49. *See also* Gonads
Respiratory system, *49,* 49–52
Ruby-throated Hummingbird, 5, *30,* 31, *31,* 42, 60, 62, 65, 87, *88–89,* 98, 99, 103, *109,* 119, 120, 141, 142, *147, 153, 154, 155–57,* 161, *164, 167, 185, 187*
Ruby-topaz Hummingbird, 40, 63
Rufous-breasted Hermit Hummingbird, 62
Rufous Hummingbird, 7, *32,* 33, *33,* 65, *66, 83, 86,* 98, 103, 108–9, 140, 141, 143, *150, 180,* 183, *183, 190, 194, 195*
Rufous-tailed Hummingbird, 5

Sap, 135
Scratching, 165, 168
Sexual organs. *See* Gonads

Skeletal system, *38,* 52–53
Skins, sale of, 59–60
Slotting, 86
Small intestine, 42, 46
Smell, 53, 140
Songs, 151–52
Sounds. *See also* Voice courtship, 104–5
Spatule-tail Hummingbird, 65
Speed, 98–99
Spinal cord, 48
Stephens, F., 151
Stomach, 42
Streamertail Hummingbird, 64
Stretching, 169, *170*
Sugar, 139–40
Sunbathing, 168
Sword-billed Hummingbird, 39
Syrinx, 57

Tail feathers (rectrices), 64–65
Taste, 53
Temperature, body, 41, 141, 143, 148
Territorial behavior, 152, 154, *155–60,* 161, *162*
Territorial hummingbirds, 140
Testes, 48
Third eyelid, *44,* 45
Thymus, 45, 46
Thyroid, 45
Tongue, 54, *54,* 56
Torpor, 138, 139, 141, 143, *143,* 145, *146–47,* 148, 149
Touch, 56
Trachea, 50, 57
Traplining hummingbirds, 140
Trochilidae, 1

Ureters, 57
Urogenital system, *56*
Urological system, 56–57
Uropygial gland, 46

Ventriculus, 42
Vervain Hummingbird, 111, 151
Violet-crowned Hummingbird, *34,* 35, *35,* 39, *196, 199*
Violet-ear Hummingbird, 99
Voice, 57, 151

Warraus, 2
Water, 135
Wedge-tail Sabrewing Hummingbird, 151
Weight loss, during torpidity, 148
White-eared Hummingbird, *36,* 37, *37, 39, 69, 81, 84, 94,* 116, 119, *162, 179, 196*
Wildflowers. *See* Flowers
Wine-throated Hummingbird, 151
Wings, 53, 140
    beating of, in flight, 96–98
    in flight, 85–87
Wing tips, 63–64
Winthrop, John, 5